PLANTS & GARDENS

BROOKLYN BOTANIC GARDEN RECORD

American Gardens:

A Traveler's Guide

1986

Brooklyn Botanic Garden

Staff for this issue:

CLAIRE E. SAWYERS, *Guest Editor*

BARBARA B. PESCH, *Editor*

CHARLES GABELER, *Art Director*

JO KEIM, *Assistant Editor*

and the Editorial Committee of the Brooklyn Botanic Garden

RUSSELL MOORE, *Director of Marketing*

DONALD E. MOORE, *President, Brooklyn Botanic Garden*

ELIZABETH SCHOLTZ, *Vice President, Brooklyn Botanic Garden*

PLANTS & GARDENS
BROOKLYN BOTANIC GARDEN RECORD

American Gardens:

A Traveler's Guide

Vol. 42   1986   No. 3

CONTENTS

Brooklyn Botanic Garden's Osborn Section in Spring .... *Elvin McDonald* Cover

Brooklyn Botanic Garden Record, Plants and Gardens (ISSN 0362-5850) is published quarterly at 1000 Washington Ave., Brooklyn, N.Y. 11225, by the **Brooklyn Botanic Garden, Inc.** Second-class-postage paid at Brooklyn, N.Y., and at additional mailing offices. Subscriptions included in Botanic Garden membership dues ($20.00 per year) which includes newletters and announcements. Copyright ©1986, 1988 by the Brooklyn Botanic Garden, Inc.
POSTMASTER: Send address changes to BROOKLYN BOTANIC GARDEN, Brooklyn, N.Y. 11225

About the Guest Editor

Claire E. Sawyers has traveled from coast to coast visiting public gardens in the United States. She holds masters' degrees in horticulture from Purdue University and the University of Delaware where she was a Fellow in the Longwood Graduate Program. She has also worked at gardens in Belgium, France and Japan, and has published many magazine articles on horticultural topics and is employed at Mt. Cuba Center in Greenville, DE. She was guest editor of Plants & Gardens *handbook* Japanese Gardens *in 1985.*

Acknowledgements

Many people made this handbook possible so that individual thanks would cover pages. However, I wish to express my thanks to the Longwood Foundation which funded my Fellowship in the Longwood Program, allowing me to do the research leading to this handbook. Thanks also go to the following widely traveled professionals, each of whom made valuable recommendations regarding entry choices:

Dr. William Barrick, Vice President, Director of Gardens
Callaway Gardens, Pine Mountain, GA

Mr. Francis Ching, Director
Department of Arboreta and Botanic Gardens, Arcadia, CA

Mr. Alan Cook, Horticulturist, and others from The Dawes Arboretum, Newark, OH

Dr. Harrison Flint, Professor, Department of Horticulture,
Purdue University, W. Lafayette, IN

Ms. Sue Lathrop, Executive Director
American Association of Botanical Gardens and Arboreta, Swarthmore, PA

Dr. Richard Lighty, Director
Mt. Cuba Center for the Study of Piedmont Flora, Greenville, DE

Dr. J.C. Raulston, Professor, Department of Horticultural Science,
North Carolina State University, Raleigh, NC

Mrs. Doris Stone, Author, and former Director of Education,
Brooklyn Botanic Garden, Brooklyn, NY

Mr. Mark Zelonis, Director
Blithewold Gardens and Arboretum, Bristol, RI

This handbook would not have been possible without the cooperation and response of each of the gardens included. Special thanks go to the staffs of each of these gardens for answering questionnaires and generously providing information brochures and photographs.

Claire Sawyers

Letter from the Brooklyn Botanic Garden

The first American Gardens—A Traveler's Guide *in the* Plants & Gardens *handbook series was published in October 1970. It remained in print for many years until it finally became outdated. Since that time there have been many requests for a new edition.*

Our guest editor, Claire E. Sawyers, researched the following information for her thesis for the Longwood Graduate Program (see preceding page). From that material our editorial committee selected the botanic gardens and arboreta to be included in this handbook. Space restrictions prevented the inclusion of all *America's public gardens, since that number has been escalating rapidly in recent years. In addition gardens in Canada could not be included because of space constraints.*

Each garden has its season for spectacular displays. For example, the highest visitation period at BBG is in late April or early May when the Kwanzan cherries transform the esplanade into a land of pink enchantment. However, at any season there will be points of interest. Even in winter, gardens located in northern climes have much to offer—characteristics of trees and shrubs that are obscured by leaves become apparent in this season. Fall in many parts of the country produces an extravagance of color in leaves, fruits and berries. And spring—whenever it occurs—bursts forth with bulbs and blossoms. Regardless of the season each garden presents its own special visual pleasures.

No matter when you plan your visit to a garden we hope this handbook will make the trip easier and more enjoyable.

Wherever you travel—enjoy!

Barbara B. Pesch
Editor

How to use this handbook

Some 250 gardens are described in this handbook, and while they range from cemeteries to botanical gardens, municipal parks to historic gardens, they are all open to the public on a regular basis and they all feature horticultural display gardens.

The gardens are organized by state, with the states listed alphabetically for easy reference. Within each state, gardens are listed alphabetically by city, then by name. If you know a garden's name but don't know its location, refer to the Index.

At the start of each entry, basic visitor information is outlined: the hours the garden is open, whether or not an admission fee is charged, directions to the garden and information about public transportation. Admission fees range from a voluntary donation to the cost of a dinner at a moderately priced restaurant. Since these fees may change on an annual basis, the exact amounts currently charged have not been included. Call the garden if you'd like to know its admission-payment policy.

At the close of each description, the services available to visitors are listed according to the following symbols:

▮ –Brochures and/or self-guiding pamphlets are available.

P –Car parking space is available in the garden proper.

♿ –Handicapped visitors can be accommodated by the walkways in at least a part of the garden, if not all.

▽ –Labels appear on at least some, if not all, plants.

✦ –Picnic facilities are available.

◗ –Restaurant or snack bar is on the premises.

▮ –A gift shop is included in the garden.

G/T –Guided tours are available. In most cases these must be arranged in advance. In some instances guided tours are restricted to groups. Call for details.

? –A visitor, orientation or education center is open to the public and provides displays or interpretive information about the garden.

Additional services provided by various gardens include membership, plant sales, educational events and motor or tram tours.

Bok Tower Gardens, Lakes Wales, Florida

Alabama

Donald E. Davis Arboretum

Auburn University (205) 826-5755
Auburn, AL 36830

Hours: every day sunrise-sunset.
Admission: no fee.
Directions: 50 mi. east of Montgomery,
I-85 to U.S. 29 north (toward Auburn); 4
mi. from I-85 at the intersection of U.S. 29
and Garden Dr.

The Davis Arboretum is a 14-acre site
planted with over 200 different kinds of
plants, mostly trees native to Alabama. The site
is used for university studies and conservation.

A vinery of native climbers and plant collections indigenous to sand, alkaline Black Belt
prairie, coastal bog and swamp habitats are
featured.

The Arboretum was established in 1963.

Birmingham Botanical Garden

2612 Lane Park Road (205) 879-1227
Birmingham, AL 35223

Hours: every day sunrise-sunset.
Admission: no fee.
Directions: 2612 Lane Park Rd., 2 blocks
from Mountain Brook Village; just off Hwy.
280 and the Red Mountain Expwy.
Public Transportation: accessible by transit
system.

The Birmingham Botanical Garden, a
municipally owned facility administered by
the Birmingham Park and Recreation Board,
was established in 1962. The 67½-acre garden, supported by 19 clubs and societies, displays over 1,500 kinds of plants.

The formal Rose Garden is made up of
2,000 individual specimens. Iris and daylily
gardens contain award-winning varieties. The
Wildflower Garden, in a former rock quarry,
features Alabama wildflowers. Hybrid and
native azaleas can be found in the Rhododendron Garden. Worldwide representatives of
hardy ferns and their close relatives grow in
the Fern Glade. Crape myrtle, the official
flower of Birmingham, is featured in one area,
while magnolias dominate another. The Garden for Southern Living shows how to revital-
ize older plantings by integrating them into a
new design. The Vegetable Garden displays
new cultivars, including All-America
Selections.

The 7½-acre Japanese Garden, designed by
a Japanese architect and completed in 1967,
contains a teahouse which was originally built
for the New York World's Fair in 1965 as a gift
of the Japanese Government.

The conservatory, and greenhouses covering 22,000 sq. ft., is one of the largest such
installations in the southeast. Camellias, desert plants, a wide variety of bromeliads,
orchids and ferns are featured inside.

Jasmine Hill Gardens

P.O. Box 6001 (205) 263-1440
Montgomery, AL 36106 567-6362

Hours: Tues.–Sun. 9–5.
Admission: fee charged.
Directions: U.S. 231 north of Montgomery
to Jasmine Hill Rd. to Gardens.

Jasmine Hill Gardens, "Alabama's little corner of Greece," features a collection of Greek
statuary in a 17-acre garden setting. Started privately in the 1920s, today the site is a public
attraction and center for the performing arts.

Fountains, pools, stairways and hedges are
accented with nearly 40 pieces of statuary,
both original and copies, including a
reproducton of the Temple of Hera, one of the
oldest of Greek temples.

Bellingrath Gardens and Home

Route 1, Box 60 (205) 973-2217
Theodore, AL 36582

Hours: every day 7–dusk; house tours start
at 8 a.m.

Oriental-American Garden at Bellingrath Gardens and Home, Theodore, Alabama

Admission: fee charged; additional fee for tour of the Home.
Directions: 20 mi. south of Mobile, exit I-10 or U.S. 90 at Theodore; take Bellingrath Hwy. to Gardens.

Bellingrath Gardens and Home, located on 65 acres overlooking the Isle-aux-Oies River, was built in the 1920s as the private estate of Walter and Bessie Bellingrath. Today, the display gardens contain 500 different kinds of plants, and the 15-room house is furnished with antiques and art objects. Just inside the entrance to the grounds, visitors come upon the Rose Garden, with over 20 beds. The central path through the Rose Garden leads to the Exotica Conservatory (1,500 sq. ft.).

Another section of the Garden centers around Mirror Lake. A terrace, summer house, rockery with bubbling pool, rustic bridge and masses of flowers surround the lake. The Oriental-American Garden features pools of water dotted with bridges and other garden structures. Opposite this is the Trial Garden.

Featured plants include live oaks, hundreds of camellias and more than 250,000 azaleas. Some 125,000 tulips and other bulbs fill the flower beds in spring. All-America Selections annuals follow and in the fall; over 60,000 chrysanthemums dominate.

The estate was opened to the public in 1932. In 1950 the Bellingrath-Morse Foundation, a not-for-profit organization, was formed to perpetuate the gardens.

Arizona

The Arboretum at Flagstaff

P.O. Box 670   **(602) 774-1441**
Flagstaff, AZ 86002

Hours: Mon.–Fri. 10–3.
Admission: no fee.
Directions: On Woody Mountain Rd. (U.S. Forest Service Rd. 230) 4 mi. south of junction of Old U.S. 66.

The 200-acre Arboretum is the only facility of its type in the Rocky Mountain West to be located above 6,000 feet elevation. It is devoted primarily to native plant propagation. Established in 1981, the Arboretum aims to serve as a resource for southwestern municipalities, developers and gardeners. The facilities include a passive solar greenhouse, research areas and offices. The first plantings were installed in 1983.

Desert Botanical Garden

1201 North Galvin Parkway   **(602) 941-1225**
Phoenix, AZ 85008

Hours: every day 9–sunset; 7–sunset during July and Aug.
Admission: fee charged.
Directions: located in Papago Park on Galvin Pkwy. between Van Buren St. and McDowell Rd.
Public Transportation: accessible by City Bus 3E (marked "Zoo").

The Desert Botanical Garden is dedicated to the study of desert and arid-land plants. Since its founding by the Arizona Cactus and Native

Outdoor Cactus Garden, Boyce Thompson Southwestern Arboretum, Superior, Arizona

Flora Society in 1939, the Garden's purpose has been to study and conserve plants of these categories. Twenty of the site's 140 acres are open to the public, and display 1,800 species, including more than 1,000 kinds of cacti. Plants native to Arizona, Australia, Baja California, plus kinds mentioned in the Bible, are featured. Of particular concern to the Garden is the study of agaves.

Boyce Thompson Southwestern Arboretum

Box AB   **(602) 689-2811**
Superior, AZ 85273

Hours: every day 8–5:30, except Dec. 25.
Admission: fee charged.
Directions: located 3 mi. west of Superior on U.S. Hwy. 60.

The Boyce Thompson Southwestern Arboretum, cooperatively managed by the Arizona State Park Board, the University of Arizona and the Arboretum Board, is a living museum of desert plants. The Arboretum encompasses 300 acres, 30 of which are open to the public.

An outstanding collection of cacti and other succulents, a notable collection of eucalyptus and other mature arid-land specimens, such as Boojum Trees *(Idria columnaris),* form a portion of the 1,440 taxa grown. A network of trails leads visitors through the Australian area (Native Trees and Shrubs, Eucalyptus Grove, Palm Grove) Olives, Pines, Cactus Garden (Yucca and Agave, Natural Desert and Natural Riparian areas). The High Trail up the Queen Creek Canyon provides views of the gardens below.

The Arboretum was the dream of Colonel William Boyce Thompson, a successful businessman in the copper mining industry. He lived at the foot of Picket Post Mountain for nearly a decade, building his winter home and developing the Arboretum. The site was chartered in 1927 and formally dedicated in 1929.

California

Los Angeles State and County Arboretum

301 N. Baldwin Avenue   (213) 446-8251
Arcadia, CA 91006

Hours: every day 9–5, except Dec. 25.
Admission: fee charged, except on the third
Tues. of every month.
Directions: 210 Frwy. to Baldwin Ave.;
south off-ramp to the Arboretum.
Public Transportation: accessible by bus.

The Los Angeles State and County Arboretum (LASCA) contains a collection of over 5,000 kinds of plants, both old favorites and new introductions, a historic preservation and a bird sanctuary. The 127-acre garden, like Sun Coast Botanic Garden and Descanso Gardens, is affiliated with the Los Angeles County Department of Arboreta and Botanic Gardens. It was founded in 1948 by the County and the California Arboretum Foundation.

Plants are grouped according to their geographic origins. Sections include South American, Mediterranean, South African, Australian and Asiatic-North American. Other displays of interest are the Aquatic Garden, Meadowbrook, Demonstration Home Gardens, Garden for All Seasons, Prehistoric and Jungle Garden, Native Oaks, Herb Garden and Palm and Bamboo collection.

In the historic area the ornate 1885 Queen Anne cottage, coach barn, restored adobe ranch house, Santa Anita Depot and Indian Wickiups are surrounded by the old-fashioned Rose Garden, Citrus Orchard and Historical Orchard. Another major attraction is the greenhouse complex (2,550 sq. ft.) where begonias, orchids and tropical plants are featured year-round.

Regional Parks Botanic Garden

Tilden Regional Park   (415) 841-8732
Berkeley, CA 94708

Hours: every day 10–5, except Thanksgiving Day, Dec. 25 and Jan. 1.

Admission: no fee.
Directions: from Berkeley take Spruce St. off University Ave. to Wildcat Canyon Rd; east of Berkeley.

Nestled in Wildcat Canyon in the center of Tilden Regional Park is this 9-acre botanic garden, devoted to the collection, display and preservation of native California plants. Gathered here are over 2,000 different plant taxa, representing all of the various habitats of California.

The Garden is divided into 10 sections, each corresponding to areas of the state, including Southern California, Valley, Santa Lucia, Channel Island, Franciscan, Pacific Rain Forest, Sierra, Redwood, Sea Bluff and Shasta. Noteworthy plant collections include conifers, oaks, manzanitas *(Arctostaphylos),* ceanothus, bunchgrasses, aquatics, endangered plants of California (over 200 species) and more generally, mature woody plants. The Botanic Garden was opened to the public in 1940.

University of California Botanical Garden

Centennial Drive   (415) 642-3343
Berkeley, CA 94720

Hours: every day 9–4:45, except Dec. 25.
Admission: no fee.
Directions: on Centennial Dr. in Strawberry Canyon, directly behind the main campus of the University of California, Berkeley.
Public Transportation: accessible by free shuttle bus from Berkeley.

This 30-acre university garden was founded in 1890 by the Botany Department. Today the department still administers the Garden and its displays of 9,000 plant taxa.

Outstanding collections include cacti and succulents, orchids, rhododendrons, California natives and South African plants. But plants from most of the major temperate regions of the world are represented in geographically arranged collections: Mediterranean and European, South American, Pacific Islands, New Zealand, Asian, Himalayan, Australian, Eastern North American, African Hill, New World

Desert, Mexican and Californian. Additional enjoyable sections include the Palm Garden, Japanese Pool, Herb Garden, Plants for Mankind, Orchard and Mather Redwood Grove. Three greenhouses (5,000 sq. ft.) are filled with ferns, orchids, cacti and tropical plants.

Virginia Robinson Gardens

1008 Elden Way	(213) 276-5367
Beverly Hills, CA 90210	

Hours: Tues.–Fri. by reservation only.
Admission: fee charged.
Directions: in Beverly Hills, just north of Los Angeles; see address.

Rancho Santa Ana Botanic Garden

1500 North College Avenue	(714) 625-8767
Claremont, CA 91711	

Hours: every day 8–5, except Jan. 1, July 4, Thanksgiving Day and Dec. 25.
Admission: no fee; donations encouraged.
Directions: Along Frwy. 10 take the Indian Hill exit and go about 2 mi. north to Foothill Blvd., then 3 blocks east to College Ave.; by way of Frwy. 210, travel 4.5 mi. east from the frwy.'s end along Foothill Blvd. to College Ave.

The Rancho Santa Ana Botanic Garden, a private research and educational institution founded in 1927, is devoted to the field of California flora. In 1951 the garden moved to its current 85-acre site, and presently is the largest botanic garden in the U.S. to focus on plants native to California. The collection consists of about 1,500 species and cultivars. On the Indian Hill Mesa portion of the grounds, plants are displayed to emphasize their ornamental value, while remaining collections consist of plants collected from the wild, documented and grouped according to 19 botanical categories. The Garden is one of 16 designed as centers for study relating to threatened and endangered plants.

Highlights include the desert garden containing cactus species: the coastal garden featuring plants from the state's shoreline; Woodland and Riparian Trails through a cool oak forest and along streams and ponds; the manzanita display area and the conifer and ceanothus collections. A spectacular display of California wildflowers carpets the mesa from mid-March through May.

Sherman Library and Gardens

2647 E. Coast Highway	(714) 673-2261
Corona Del Mar, CA 92625	

Hours: Gardens, every day 10:30–4; Library, Mon.–Fri. 9–5; Garden Shop, every day 10:30–3:30; closed Thanksgiving Day, Dec. 25 and Jan. 1.
Admission: fee charged every day but Mon.
Directions: located 40 mi. south of Los Angeles; take frwy. to Irvine; exit at MacArthur Blvd.; follow MacArthur south to Coast Hwy.; turn left, go one block.
Public Transportation: accessible by Rapid Transit Bus.

University of California Arboretum—Davis

Department of Botany	(916) 752-2498
University of California	
Davis, CA 95616	

Hours: grounds, year-round, all hours; Arboretum office, Mon.–Fri. 8–5, except holidays.
Admission: no fee.
Directions: just north of I–80, on the University of California campus at Davis; Arboretum office on La Rue Rd., across from campus parking lot #46.

The University of California Arboretum is a 110-acre, 2-mile strip of land flanking both banks of the Putah Creek. Affiliated with the University's Department of Botany, the

Arboretum contains about 1,500 kinds of plants.

The Acacia Section contains 80 different acacia species; the Shields Grove area is devoted to oaks (75 species); the Exotic Conifer Section to cone-bearing trees from foreign countries; the Native Plant Section to plants from the Sierra Nevada and Coast Ranges; the Desert Section to plants from the southwest; the Exotic Section to woody plants from Australia, South Africa and the Mediterranean region (eucalyptus trees are prominent). Also featured is a redwood grove planted in 1941.

The Arboretum was started in 1936 by staff and students of the University. Numerous California species were planted in 1940–41, and in 1968–69 an extensive development project was carried out.

Quail Botanical Gardens ✕

230 Quail Gardens Drive	(714) 753-4432
Encinitas, CA 92024	436-3036

Hours: in winter, every day 8–5; in summer, 8–6.
Admission: no fee; parking fee charged.
Directions: 27 mi. north of San Diego off I–5; take Encinitas Blvd. ¼ mi. east of Quail Gardens Dr.

About half of the Quail Botanical Gardens' 30 acres is a display garden, while the other half is a wildlife sanctuary. Nearly 3,000 kinds of tropical, subtropical, and California native plants can be found here. The installation was originally the private estate of Ruth Baird Larabee, until 1957 when she donated her house and 27 acres to the County of San Diego. The Quail Botanical Gardens Foundation was established in 1961.

Plant groups emphasized include fuchsias, hibiscus, bamboos (Quail Botanical Gardens is an official test facility for these plants), proteas, cacti and succulents, and other drought-tolerant plants such as Australian shrubs. Herbs, water plants, wildflowers, South American and Australian perennials, brugmansias, cork oaks and palms are also featured. The Mildred MacPherson Waterfall is one of the most popular spots in the garden, and buildings dating from 1850 to 1920 add a historic atmosphere. These include Encinitas's first meeting hall, first schoolhouse and the Larabee residence.

Ficus *trees at South Coast Botanic Garden, Palo Verdes, California (photo: William Aplin)*

13

Mendocino Coast Botanical Gardens

18220 N. Highway 1	(707) 964-4352
Fort Bragg, CA 95437	

Hours: in winter, every day 8:30–5; in summer, 8:30–6; closed holidays.
Admission: fee charged.
Directions: 1 mi. south of Ft. Bragg, 6 mi. north of Mendocino on Hwy. 1.

Fullerton Arboretum

California State	(714) 773-3579
University, Fullerton	
800 N. State College	
Boulevard	
Fullerton, CA 92634	

Hours: every day 8–4:45, except Dec. 25 through Jan. 1 and other major holidays; Heritage House is open for guided tours Sun. 2–4; closed August.
Admission: no fee for grounds: fee charged

East Garden, the J. Paul Getty Museum, Malibu, California (photo: Julius Shulman)

for Heritage House.
Directions: located at the northeast corner of California State University, Fullerton; adjacent to Frwy. 57 at Yorba Linda Blvd; entrance from Associated Rd.
Public Transportation: accessible by bus.

Fullerton Arboretum has three stated purposes: to create a quiet retreat in a rapidly growing urban area; to provide California State University and the local community with a resource for environmental and historical education, and to conserve natural resources. The 26-acre site was opened to the public in 1979, following 10 years of development.

Plants are arranged according to their habitat requirements. A stream and ponds provide moisture for evergreen conifers, deciduous trees, tropicals and bog plants. Arid environments include oak woodlands, chaparral, deserts and thorn scrub. Other points of interest are the Palm Grove, Rare Fruit Grove, rose gardens and community gardens.

The Heritage House area is the focal point of the Arboretum. The House, built in 1894, has been carefully restored and is surrounded by structures and gardens typical of the 1890s.

Blake Garden

Location address:
70 Ricon Road
Kensington, CA 94707

Mailing address:
2 Norwood Place
Kensington, CA 94707
(415) 524-2449

Hours: weekdays 9–4:30; closed weekends and holidays.
Admission: no fee.
Directions: in Kensington, which is north of Berkeley, across the bay from San Francisco.
Public Transportation: accessible by bus.

Descanso Gardens

1418 Descanso Drive
La Canada, CA 91011
(213) 790-5571

Hours: every day 9–5, except Dec. 25.
Admission: fee charged except on the third Tues. of every month.
Directions: located in La Canada-Flintridge, near the junction of Frwy. 210 and Rt. 2
Public Transportation: accessible by bus.

Descanso Gardens, built on 160 acres of native chaparral-covered slopes (80 acres are open as a display garden), is operated by the Los Angeles County Department of Arboreta and Botanic Gardens.

Descanso has "the largest plantings of camellias in the world," with thousands of specimens, representing over 600 varieties. A forest of California live oaks forms a canopy over the plantings of camellias and azaleas. Roses fill a 5-acre section. Other areas include the Cymbidium Orchid Dell, Fern Dell, California Native Plants and plantings of day-lilies. Near the entrance of the grounds is the Oriental Tea House, surrounded by a garden donated by the Japanese-American community. Hospitality House, with adjoining Meditation Garden, is a 1939 mansion, the original residence of the Garden's builder.

In 1957 a group of citizens formed the Descanso Gardens Guild to protect and promote the gardens.

Mildred E. Mathias Botanical Garden

University of California
Los Angeles, CA 90045
(213) 825-2714

Hours: weekdays 8–5; weekends 8–4; closed University holidays.
Admission: no fee.
Directions: from San Diego Frwy. (I–405) to Wilshire Blvd.; east on Wilshire to Westwood Blvd. and north. Upon entering the campus, Westwood becomes Westwood Plaza. At kiosk, obtain parking permit (fee charged). The Garden is at the southeast corner of the campus and is bordered by Hilgard and Le Conte Aves.
Public Transportation: accessible by bus.

The Mildred E. Mathias Botanical Garden, displaying 4,000 kinds of plants, is set in a natural canyon with a stream running through it. It features a wide variety of subtropical ornamental trees and shrubs and many unusual species not commonly seen in the California landscape. Australian, desert, and Acanthus-Family plants, palms, cycads and native plants are emphasized collections. The UC Biology Department started the Garden in 1929.

The J. Paul Getty Museum

17985 Pacific Coast Highway
Malibu, CA 90265
(213) 459-2306
458-2003

Hours: Tues.–Sun. 10–5; closed Dec. 25, July 4, Jan. 1 and Thanksgiving Day.
Admission: no fee; make parking reservations at least one week in advance, at no charge; due to an agreement with local residents, pedestrians are not permitted into the museum. Bus passengers may obtain a museum pass from the driver.
Public Transportation: accessible by RTD bus line #434.

The J. Paul Getty Museum, housed in a re-creation of the Villa dei Papiri, is surrounded by five gardens based on excavations of the 1st-century A.D. villa. When Mr. Getty's art collection outgrew his Malibu mansion, he built the villa to house his Greek and Roman antiquities, Renaissance and Baroque paintings, and decorative arts. The building opened in 1974, two years before his death.

In the Main Peristyle Garden, a long reflecting pool and bronze statues, based on the originals excavated from the villa, are framed by clipped shrubbery and trees. Next door lies the Herb Garden. In the smaller East and West and Inner Peristyle Gardens, fountains and wall frescoes are featured with the plantings. The 1,000 trees, shrubs, flowers and herbs used in the design are kinds that might have been growing in the original villa.

The Living Desert

47-900 Portola Avenue   (619) 346-5694
P.O. Box 1775
Palm Desert, CA 92261

Hours: every day 9–5, except June–August.
Admission: fee charged.
Directions: from Los Angeles (150 mi.) east on I–10 to Bob Hope Dr. exit; south on Bob Hope Dr. to Hwy. 111 to Portola Ave. (in Palm Desert); south 1½ mi.
Public Transportation: accessible by bus.

The Living Desert, an ecological preserve and interpretive center, offers live animal exhibits, botanical gardens and nature trails. Nine hundred acres of the 1,300-acre reserve are open to the public; 500 kinds of desert plants are displayed on 25 acres devoted to gardens. A variety of North American desert-type plants is represented in the Agave Garden, Mojave Garden, Lower Colorado Sand Dune, Upper Colorado Garden, Opuntia Garden, Baja Garden and Indian Garden. In the Indian Garden visitors learn how desert plants were used by local native Americans.

Visitors may explore the natural areas, spread over six miles of trails up Eisenhower

Mountain and into a canyon. Wildflowers bloom from January to May. The preserve was established in 1952 by Philip Boyd.

South Coast Botanic Garden

26300 Crenshaw Blvd.   (213) 772-5813
Palo Verdes Peninsula,
CA 90274

Hours: every day 9–5, except Dec. 25.
Admission: fee charged, except on the third Tues. of every month.
Directions: from Los Angeles take Harbor Frwy. to Pacific Coast Hwy. (101) west to Crenshaw Blvd.; south on Crenshaw about 1 mi.

South Coast Botanic Garden sits on 3½ million tons of refuse covered with topsoil. It is one of the first botanic gardens to be developed over a sanitary landfill. The 87-acre site, first planted in 1961, contains more than 2,000 species. The Garden is administered by the Los Angeles County Department of Arboreta and Botanic Gardens.

A one-mile road circles the site, while numerous paths and walkways allow visitors to explore the inner regions. Features include the Fruiting Orchard, Shade Garden, Vegetable Display Garden and herbaceous ground covers. The Garden is particularly rich in plants from Australia, the Mediterranean and South Africa.

Filoli Center, Woodside, California (photo: Carol Ivie)

Institute of Forest Genetics
(The Eddy Arboretum)

Pacific Southwest Forest   **(916) 622-1225**
and Range Experiment Station
Forest Service,
U.S. Department
of Agriculture
2840 Carson Road
Placerville, CA 95667

Hours: Mon.–Fri. 8–4:30; closed
weekends and holidays.
Admission: no fee.
Directions: 3 mi. east of Placerville on
Carson Rd.

The Institute of Forest Genetics, operated
by the Forest Service of the U.S. Department
of Agriculture, is known internationally for
pioneering research in the hybridization of
pines. Fifteen acres of the 160-acre experiment
station offer visitors a display of conifers; pines
of the world (about 70 species) grow along the
Eddy Arboretum Trail. The arboretum was
donated to the people of the United States by
James G. Eddy in 1925.

University of California
Botanic Gardens-Riverside

Department of Botany   **(718) 787-4650**
and Plant Science
Riverside, CA 92521

Hours: every day 8–5, except Jan. 1, July 4,
Thanksgiving Day and Dec. 25.
Admission: no fee.
Directions: exit frwy. in Riverside at Univer-
sity Ave.; Gardens on the east side of
campus, off East Campus Drive, through
Parking Lot 13.

The 39-acre Botanic Gardens of the University of California at Riverside display 3,000
kinds of plants for teaching, research and public enjoyment. Featured areas include the
Cactus and Succulent Garden, Rose Garden,
Iris Garden, Herb Garden and Daylily Garden.

Southwest-Desert and Australian shrubs and
trees, plus *Ficus* species, are emphasized in the
woody plantings. In the greenhouse (3,000 sq.
ft.; open upon request), cycads are prominent.
The Gardens were established in 1963.

San Diego Zoo

P.O. Box 551   **(714) 231-1515**
San Diego, CA 92112   **234-3153**

Hours: July to Labor Days everyday 9–5;
otherwise 9–4
Admission: fee charged (group rates avail-
able); free on Founder's Day in Oct.
Directions: in Balboa Park, just east of Rt.
163; Wild Animal Park* is about 30 mi.
north of downtown San Diego via I–15
(Hwy. 163); exit via Rancho Pkwy. to San
Pasqual Rd.; follow signs.
Public Transportation: accessible by bus.

The San Diego Zoo's 3,200 animals (800
species) are displayed in a 100-acre tropical-
garden setting; most are contained in moated
enclosures that approximate the animals'
native habitats. Major plant collections are
tropical, subtropical and warm tropical,
including cycads, aloes, figs, palms, bamboo,
ferns, orchids, bromeliads, euphorbias,
erythrinas, eucalyptus, South African bulbs,
bananas and tropical conifers. The Zoo also
serves as an official test garden for local landscape introductions. In the Zoo and surrounding Balboa Park, over 5,000 plant species are
grown.

*The Zoo also maintains Wild Animal Park,
a 1,800-acre sanctuary. Conservation is the
primary goal here and animals roam freely
in natural settings. Visitors may observe them
from a monorail train or from a hiking trail.
Hours: June 21 to Labor Day, Mon.–Thurs.
9–6; Fri.–Sun. 9–8; Labor Day to June 20,
9–4. Call (619) 234-6541, 480-0100 or
747-8702 for further information.

Sea World of California

1720 S. Shores Road   (619) 226-3901
San Diego, CA 92109

Hours: every day 9–dusk; June to Labor Day 9–11.
Admission: fee charged.
Directions: take Sea World Drive exit off I–5 or take E. Mission Bay Drive exit off I–8 to Sea World Drive.
Public Transportation: accessible by San Diego Transit; call (619) 233-3004 for routes and schedules.

Sea World is a marine zoological park presenting six shows and thirty educational exhibits. It also features over 4,000 species of plants on its 135-acre landscaped site. Horticultural highlights include planted water areas (where one of the largest water-fowl collections in the U.S. can be seen), the Japanese Garden (with a reproduction of Kyoto's Golden Pavilion), the Trough Garden (containing many alpine plants) and the Rock Garden (small plants, ground covers, dwarf conifers, palms, cycads, bamboos and ferns). Annuals and perennials flower throughout the year.

Most of the plants in the park were selected for their ability to withstand a salt-laden, seaside environment. Sea World opened to the public in 1964.

Japanese Teahouse, Descanso Gardens, La Canada, California (photo: Bobby Vargas)

Conservatory of Flowers—Golden Gate Park

Location:	Mailing Address:
J.F. Kennedy Dr.	McLaren Lodge
San Francisco, CA	Fell and Stanyan Streets
(415) 558-3973	San Francisco, CA 94117

Hours: Apr.–Oct. every day 9–6; other times 9–5.
Admission: fee charged, except on the first Wed. of each month, major holidays and from 9–9:30.
Directions: Conservatory is in Golden Gate Park, ½ mi. west of Stanyan St. at the beginning of the Park. Take Fell St. exit from U.S. 101; 2 mi. south of Bay Bridge.
Public Transportation: accessible by #5 Fulton bus.

Within the 1,000-acre Golden Gate Park is the Conservatory of Flowers, a Victorian structure erected in 1879. In the historic structure's 11,000 sq. ft. under glass, about 4,500 kinds of plants are grown. Restoration of the Conservatory's decorative details was undertaken in 1983.

Tropical plant collections include begonias, gesneriads, bromeliads, orchids, aroids, carnivors, palms, cycads and ferns. In addition to the permanent installations, seasonal floral displays are featured year-round.

Hearst Castle, San Simeon, California

those from areas of similar climate, namely Australia, New Zealand, South Africa, central Chile and the Asiatic cloud forest. Rare rhododendrons and magnolias are featured among the 5,000 species grown. Individual gardens include the Garden of Fragrance, Succulent Garden, Conifer Garden, Biblical Garden and demonstration gardens for the homeowner. Construction of the Arboretum began in 1937.

Strybing Arboretum and Botanical Gardens

Ninth Avenue at Lincoln Way   (415) 558-3622
San Francisco, CA 94122

Hours: weekdays 8–4:30; weekends and holidays 10–5.
Admission: no fee.
Directions: Hwy. 1 north; turn right at Lincoln Way.
Public Transportation: MUNI Metro north to Ninth Avenue.

Strybing Arboretum and Botanical Gardens, located in San Francisco's Golden Gate Park, benefits from the Mediterranean climate of coastal California. Featured plants include

Hungtington Botanical Gardens

1151 Oxford Road   (818) 405-2100
San Marino, CA 91108

Hours: Tues.–Sun. 1–4:30 (Sun. by advance-ticket reservation only; write or call ahead of time); closed Mon. and major holidays; Art Gallery and Library open the same hours.
Admission: no fee; suggested contribution.
Directions: 1½ mi. south on Allen Ave. from Foothill Frwy. (210) in Pasadena. Exit Allen Ave. (if coming from the east); exit Hill Ave. (if from the west) and take access road to Allen Ave.; 12 mi. northeast of downtown Los Angeles.

Public Transportation: accessible by bus; stop within 3–4 blocks.

The one-time private estate of the Henry E. Huntingtons is today a place of learning and beauty. The library houses 600,000 books of American and English history and literature, while the Art Gallery contains the most comprehensive collection of 18th- and 19th-century British art outside London. A dozen display gardens contain over 15,000 different kinds of plants. About 130 of the 207 acres are open to the public.

The North Vista, directly north of the Art Gallery, is an expanse of lawn lined with azaleas, camellias, palms and 17th-century Italian statuary. The Shakespeare Garden contains an acre of plants that were cultivated in English gardens during Shakespeare's time. The Rose Garden has more than 1,000 varieties arranged historically. The five-acre Japanese Garden features the 19th-century Japanese house, temple bell and pavilion, moon bridge, and bonsai court. The Zen Garden, of sand, was added in the 1960s. The 12-acre Desert Garden, with 5,000 species, is the "largest outdoor collection of desert plants in the world." Another expansive collection is devoted to camellias (1,500 varieties). In the Palm Garden about 200 mature specimens can be seen, and in the Australian Garden over 100 varieties of eucalyptus are grown, along with acacias and bottlebrushes.

In 1903 Henry E. Huntington bought working ranchland sparsely covered with native vegetation. During the next 24 years he turned it into lush gardens and a haven for scholars.

Hearst Castle
(Hearst San Simeon State Historical Monument)

P.O. Box 8   (805) 927-4622
San Simeon, CA 93452

Hours: every day 8:30–3, except Thanksgiving Day, Dec. 25 and Jan. 1.
Admission: fee charged; reservations recommended.
Directions: located just off California Scenic Hwy. 1, east of San Simeon; from San Francisco take Hwy. 101, exit 46 west, 2 mi. after Paso Robles; north on Hwy. 1 for 45 mi.

William Randolph Hearst (1863-1951) created La Cuesta Encantada (The Enchanted Hill) with acres of gardens, terraces, pools, palatial guest houses and the 137-foot tall, 100-room Hispano-Mooresque mansion, Casa Grande. He started construction in 1919 on the then-240,000-acre family ranch. Today, the estate is owned and operated by the State of California, Department of Parks and Recreation. The property contains one of the nation's outstanding collections of art objects and five acres of gardens.

Prominent plants in the landscape include Italian cypress, palms and California native live oaks. Oleanders, citrus, pomegranates, persimmons, quince, roses, camellias, rhododendrons, perennials and annuals are also found in the formal and informal gardens surrounding the buildings.

Santa Barbara Botanic Garden

1212 Mission Canyon Road   (805) 682-4726
Santa Barbara, CA 93105

Hours: every day 8–sunset.
Admission: no fee.
Directions: 3 mi. north of Santa Barbara; Rt. 101 to Los Olivos St., turn right on Mission Canyon Rd. behind the Old Mission and follow the signs.

Santa Barbara Botanic Garden is a picturesque 65-acre display garden devoted to California native flora. Plants from the deserts, grasslands and offshore islands are arranged in naturalistic settings. Five miles of trails lace the area. Special attractions include the Ceanothus Section, the Meadow Section with massive live oaks and a water garden, the Desert Section (colorful in early summer) and a Redwood Grove bordering the creek. Plants from offshore islands are offered in the Island Section in the lower canyon. The installation dates from 1926 when Anna Bliss founded it as a public display garden.

UCSC Arboretum

University of California
Santa Cruz, CA 95064

Hours: Wed. and weekends 2–4.
Admission: no fee.
Directions: located on campus; entrance on Empire Grade ¼ mi. northwest of the Empire Grade and Western Dr. intersection.
Public Transportation: accessible by metropolitan bus.

The UCSC Arboretum specializes in woody plants of unusual scientific interest and ornamental shrubs from regions with mild climates. Half of the 80 acres open to the public display about 4,000 different types of plants.

At the Elevenia J. Slosson Research Gardens, also on campus, is an excellent selection of Australian ornamentals. The Gardens are the result of an extensive program of importing material, and they change continually as new introductions are added. They now contain over 1,000 cultivars.

Three greenhouses (1,500 sq. ft.), primarily used for propagation, are also open to the public.

Gazebo and Water Lily Pool, Denver Botanic Gardens, Denver, Colorado

Hakone Japanese Garden

21000 Big Basin Way   **(408) 867-3438**
Saratoga, CA 95070

Hours: Mon.–Fri. 10–5; Sat.–Sun. 11–5; closed legal holidays.
Admission: no fee; donation requested.
Directions: Hwy. 280 to Saratoga Ave. off ramp; south on Saratoga Ave. about 5 mi. (pass through downtown area of Saratoga); Garden is on the left just outside town (Saratoga Ave. changes to Big Basin Way).

Filoli Center

Canada Road   **(415) 364-2880**
Woodside, CA 94062

Hours: mid–Feb. to mid–Nov. Tues.–Sat.
Admission: fee charged; advance reservations required; visitors must be 12 yrs. of age or older.
Directions: located 25 mi. south of San Francisco, just off Hwy. 280. Take Edgewood exit west, turn north on Canada Rd.; 1.3 mi. to the gate.

Filoli, a property of the National Trust for Historic Preservation, is a reflection of the opulent manner of living of wealthy San Franciscans Mr. and Mrs. William B. Bourn II during the early 20th century. The mansion, built between 1916 and 1919, is a definitive example of country-home architecture. It is surrounded by 16 acres of gardens originally designed by Bruce Porter and Isabella Worn. The mature plantings, buffered by more than 600 acres of wilderness, combine formal design with natural surroundings. The Walled Garden contains fountains, clipped hedges, columnar evergreens, graceful flowering trees and an Italian-Renaissance teahouse. The interior of the teahouse emphasizes container plantings. The rose garden, formal parterres, perennial and annual borders (All-America Selections), plantings of azaleas, rhododendrons, camellias and magnolias, lawns and reflecting pools form other sections of the formal garden.

To administer the property, a not-for-profit corporation, Filoli Center, was established in 1976.

Colorado

Denver Botanic Gardens

909 York Street   **(303) 575-2547**
Denver, CO 80206

Hours: every day, except Dec. 25, Jan. 1 and the Thurs. before Mother's Day.
Admission: fee charged, except during Plant and Christmas Sales.
Directions: 2½ mi. north on University (York) St. from I-25; 3½ mi. south on York from I-70.

On 22 intensively landscaped acres, Denver Botanic Gardens display 10,000 kinds of plants. The Gardens are an agency of the City and County of Denver, Department of Parks and Recreation.

The Conservatory and Orchid/Bromeliad Pavilion display over 800 tropical and subtropical plants — more than 1,000 species of orchids and 1,200 species of bromeliads. Over 13,000 sq. ft. under glass are open to the public. The one-acre rock garden is filled with alpine plants, while seasonal displays of tundra plants are found in the Alpine House. Shofu-en, a Japanese Garden with a naturalistic lake, features handcrafted bridges, gates and a teahouse. In the Herb Garden fragrant and ancient herbs are arranged in traditional bow-knot pattern.

Other specialized areas include: a simulated Rocky Mountain landscape; Landscape Demonstration Garden (illustrating low-maintenance and intensive-gardening styles); Scripture Garden; Dahlia, Iris and Daylily, Peony, Lilac, and Plains Gardens; All-America Rose Selection Test Plots; demonstration area for annuals, turf and vegetables; Juniper Mound, and a pergola dressed with vines. The various areas of the Gardens are connected by a system of waterfalls, fountains and pools.

The Gardens were founded in 1951 by a group of interested citizens. Construction began in 1959 and the plantings have been expanding ever since.

The Denver Botanic Gardens facility also oversees three additional sites: The Chatfield Arboretum, a 700-acre tract (under construction) in the foothills near Chatfield Dam and Reservoir southwest of Denver; the Walter S. Reed Botanical Garden, a 20-acre preserve located west of Denver near Evergreen in the montane zone, and Mount Goliath Alpine Unit, a 160-acre area 50 miles west of Denver with a two-mile nature trail that winds through alpine and subalpine zones. The first two are open to the public only at selected times and may be seen by contacting the main office at 909 York Street. The Alpine Unit is open during the summer months.

Connecticut

New Canaan Nature Center

144 Oenoke Ridge   **(203) 966-9577**
New Canaan, CT 06840

Hours: Tues.–Sat. 9:30–4:30; Sun. 12:30–4:30; closed Mon. and major holidays.
Admission: no fee.
Directions: ½ mi. north of New Canaan on Rt. 124.

Donated to the community, the New Canaan Nature Center was established in 1959 on the former estate of Susan Dwight Bliss. The Horticultural Education Building, a solar-heated complex with greenhouse space (3,000 sq. ft.) was added in 1983. Landscaped areas on the 40-acre property include a wildflower garden, herb garden and large perennial border.

Connecticut Arboretum

Connecticut College	(203) 447-1911
Williams Street	ext. 7700
New London, CT 06320	

Hours: every day sunrise–sunset.
Admission: no fee; information and bulletins in Botany Office, 209 New London Hall.
Directions: main entrance to Connecticut College is on the west side of Rt. 32, about 1 mi. north of I–95 in New London; cross the campus to the William St. main gate to the Arboretum.
Public Transportation: accessible by bus from downtown New London.

Along the periphery of Connecticut College's campus are several tracts of land (a total of over 400 acres) that comprise the Connecticut Arboretum. The diversity of sites has served the college as an outdoor laboratory, and the community and visitors as a park, nature study area and wildlife refuge since 1931. The Arboretum is administered by the Botany Department.

From the main entrance to the Arboretum, Laurel Walk leads visitors amid mountain laurel, down to the Arboretum Pond. Surrounding the pond is a collection of over 200 kinds of native trees and shrubs. Plantings include pines, viburnums, azaleas, hawthorns, birches, hollies, oaks and conifers. Next to the pond is the Outdoor Theater, screened with hemlock. Other points of interest include Buck Lodge (a rustic stone building used for meetings), the Edgerton Wildflower Area and the naturalistic Landscape Demonstration Area.

The Arboretum also maintains, across campus, the Caroline Black Botanic Garden. This four-acre landscaped area contains a collection of ornamental trees, shrubs and dwarf plants. Several other sites, along public roads, demonstrate vegetation management through the selective use of herbicides.

Bartlett Arboretum

The University of Connecticut	(203) 322-6971
151 Brookdale Road	
Stamford, CT 06903	

Hours: Arboretum, every day 8:30–sunset; library, weekdays 8:30–4.
Admission: no fee.
Directions: 7 mi. north of Stamford on High Ridge Rd. (Rt. 137); left onto Brookdale Rd.
Public Transportation: Conrail; bus from train station; ¼ mi. from the bus stop.

Hagley Museum and Library, Wilmington, Delaware

Bartlett Arboretum, a part of the Department of Plant Science of The University of Connecticut, functions primarily as a teaching facility for public education. The 63-acre Arboretum features the Dwarf Conifer Garden, Ericaceous Collection and small flowering trees. The facility was established in 1965 with funds from a private estate.

Harkness Memorial State Park

275 Great Neck Road   (203) 443-5725
Waterford, CT 06385

Hours: grounds, every day 8–sunset; buildings, every day, Memorial Day to Labor Day, 10–5.
Admission: fee charged.
Directions: I–95, exit 74; south on Rt. 161 to Niantic; east on Rt. 156 to Rt. 213.

Formerly the estate of Edward S. Harkness, this 125-acre site on Long Island Sound was left to the State of Connecticut in 1950. Surrounding the 42-room mansion (built in 1902) are the Italian Garden (with a water-lily pool), Oriental Garden, Cutting Garden and greenhouse complex.

Delaware

The Hagley Museum and Library   ✗

P.O. Box 3630   (302) 658-2400
Greenville,
Wilmington, DE 19807

Hours: every day 9:30–4:30, special winter hours Apr.–Dec.
Admission: fee charged.
Directions: from I–95, either Rt. 52 or Rt. 202 exits; located on Rt. 141 between Rts. 52 and 202; 1 hr. from Philadelphia.

Hagley Museum, situated along the scenic Brandywine River, offers a look at American industrial life in the 19th century. On the 230-acre site, a museum (formerly a textile mill) and original du Pont black-powder mills trace America's industrial development. Upstream lies Eleutherian Mills, the Georgian-style mansion built in the 1800s by E. I. du Pont. A garden at the front of the mansion has been restored to the period of its first cultivation by Mr. du Pont. About two acres were excavated to determine original locations of paths and garden structures, and household accounts and letters provided documentation for the 100 kinds of plants found in the garden today.

On the hillside below the mansion, the Renaissance-Revival garden created by Louise du Pont Crowninshield and her husband during the 1920's has also been stabilized. This romantic garden features terraces and statuary.

In preparing to celebrate the sesquicentennial of E. I. du Pont de Nemours and Company, family members and corporate personnel decided to preserve the historic Brandywine site. The Eleutherian Mills-Hagley Foundation was formed in 1954, and the museum opened to the public in 1957. By 1972 the plan for restoring the garden had been completed.

Nemours   ✗

Location: (302) 651-6912
Rockland Road   Mailing Address:
    Reservations Office
    P.O. Box 109
    Wilmington, DE 19899

Hours: May–Nov., Tues.–Sat.; tours at 9, 11, 1 and 3; Sun. tours at 11, 1 and 3; arrive 15 minutes before tour times.
Admission: fee charged; advance reservations highly recommended; must be at least 16 yrs. of age.
Directions: on Rockland Rd., between US Rt. 202 and St. Rt. 141.

Winterthur Museum and Gardens   ✗

Winterthur, DE 19735   (302) 654-1548

U.S. National Arboretum, Washington, D.C.

Hours: Tues.–Sat. 10–4; Sun. and holiday Mon. 12–4; otherwise closed Mon., Jan. 1, July 4, Thanksgiving Day, Dec. 24–25.
Admission: fee charged; a variety of tours.
Directions: 6 mi. northwest of Wilmington on Rt. 52; exit 7 off I–95.
Public Transportation: limited bus service from Wilmington.

Winterthur, the former home of Henry Francis du Pont, is known for its extraordinary collection of American antiques. These are displayed throughout the 196 rooms of the sprawling mansion. The 200 acres of surrounding gardens, designed by du Pont, remain one of the finest examples in this country of landscaping in the English naturalistic style. Today, the gardens as a whole typify the large country estates developed during the first half of the 20th century.

Gentle winding paths allow visitors to wander through woods, garden areas and plantings and enjoy about 4,000 different kinds of plants. Under stands of mature hardwoods in the Azalea Woods, drifts of Kurume azaleas are combined with rhododendrons, dogwoods, viburnums, bulbs and wildflowers. At the woods' edge saucer magnolias accent the landscape. The nearby Witch Hazel Area provides one of the first big spring displays, while the March Bank, covered with bulbs peaks in the month of its name. The Pinetum contains unusual specimens of conifers (more than 50 species and varieties) planted in 1914. From Oak Hill, meadows, streams, ponds and woodlands can be surveyed throughout the year.

Closer to the mansion are the Reflecting Pool Area and the Peony Garden. An abandoned quarry, developed into a naturalist garden, features native and exotic bog plants, including sweeps of primulas.

H. F. du Pont inherited Winterthur in 1927 and until his death in 1969, he developed the grounds, mansion and collections. In 1930 he established a private foundation to care for the estate.

District of Columbia

Bishop's Garden of Washington Cathedral

Mt. St. Alban   (202) 537-6200
Washington, D.C. 20016

Hours: grounds, every day sunrise–7.
Admission: no fee.
Directions: on Wisconsin Ave. NW, between Woodley Rd. and Massachusetts Ave. NW.
Public Transportation: accessible by Washington city buses.

Dumbarton Oaks

1703 32nd Street NW   (202) 338-8278
Washington, D.C. 20007

Hours: grounds, every day 2–5, except holidays; Museum, Tues.–Sun. 2–5, except holidays.
Admission: fee charged, except Nov.–Mar.
Directions: located in the northwest section of the city, in Georgetown; garden entrance at 31st and R Sts.
Public Transportation: accessible by bus; stop one block away.

Dumbarton Oaks is referred to by some as the "last great American garden." The 16 acres surrounding a Georgian-style mansion represent the creative efforts of Mrs. Beatrix Farrand, the noted landscape architect, and Mrs. Robert Woods Bliss.

From 1922 the two worked together for 25 years on the estate, perfecting the garden with the best ornamental plant materials available.

The garden comprises a series of terraces built on a hill behind the house, with the remaining areas laid out in informal plantings. Courtyard-terrace areas include the Star Garden, Green Garden, Swimming Pool, Beech Terrace, Urn Terace, formal Rose Garden, Arbor Terrace, Fountain Terrace, Lovers' Lane Pool and the Pebble Terrace. This last features a pebble mosaic of a wheat sheath glimmering under a thin layer of water. The Camellia Circle, Prunus Walk, Cherry Hill, Crabapple Hill, Forsythia Hill and Fairview Hill radiate

from the Ellipse, a circular fountain ringed by walks and clipped trees.

Mr. and Mrs. Bliss acquired Dumbarton Oaks in 1920 when they began adding to the 1801 mansion and developing the grounds. In 1940 the Blisses gave Dumbarton Oaks to Harvard University as a means of preserving the estate and collections. The gardens opened to the public soon after.

Oak Hill Cemetery

3001 R Street NW   (202) 337-2835
Washington, D.C. 20007

Hours: every day 9–5, except Sat., Sun. and national legal holidays.
Admission: no fee.
Directions: in Georgetown on R St. NW, 3 blocks east of Wisconsin Ave.; at the north end of 30th St.; a neighbor of Dumbarton Oaks.
Public Transportation: accessible by Washington Metropolitan Transit System.

The 25 acres of Oak Hill Cemetery form a naturalistic, picturesque landscape dating from the first half of the 19th century. Established by W. W. Corcoran in 1849, the garden cemetery was designed to display the ideals of Andrew Jackson Downing and the Garden Cemetery Movement. Oak Hill may be "the best surviving A. J. Downing garden."

U.S. Botanic Garden

Location Address: (202) 225-7099
Maryland Ave., SW   **Mailing Address:**
                             245 First St., SW
                             Washington, D.C. 20024

Hours: every day 9–5; June–Aug. 9–9.
Admission: no fee.
Directions: at the foot of Capitol Hill facing Maryland Ave., SW; follow exit signs on

I–295 or I–395 to the U.S. Capitol.
Public Transportation: accessible by public bus and the orange and blue subway lines.

The U.S. Botanic Garden houses a living collection of 2,000 kinds of tropical, subtropical and desert plants. The Botanic Garden is a part of the Federal Government, under the jurisdiction of the Joint Committee of the Library of Congress.

The series of 10 houses, connected to form the rectangular conservatory complex of 29,000 sq. ft., includes the Cactus, Bromeliad, Fern, Cycad and Subtropical Houses. The tallest, the Palm House, stands at the center of the complex. Orchids are displayed in the Subtropical House, with 200 to 300 blooming plants on display continuously. Most of the houses are landscaped with rocks and display the plants in a naturalistic manner.

United States National Arboretum

Agricultural Research Service   (202) 472-9279
U.S. Department of Agriculture
3501 New York Ave. NE
Washington, D.C. 20002

Hours: weekdays 8–5; weekends and holidays 10–5; closed Dec. 25.
Admission: no fee.
Directions: located in the northeast section of Washington, D.C. Take Maryland Ave. from the Capitol to Bladensburg Rd., then to New York Ave. Visitor entrance is located on New York Ave. NE.
Public Transportation: from central Washington, accessible by Metrorail or bus; call (202) 637-2437.

The National Arboretum's 49,000 plant accessions are maintained on 444 acres along the Anticostia River. Plants from a wide range of climates are grown, adding to the Arboretum's national character. Research activities involve plant introduction, breeding, selection and distribution. The Science and Education Administration, Department of Agriculture, administers the Arboretum.

Nine miles of roads connect single-genus collections, such as hollies (700 species and cultivars), crabapples (about 500 kinds), crape myrtle, dogwood (70 kinds), pyracantha, magnolias, cherries, irises, viburnums and maples. Boxwood, daylilies and peonies are planted in formal-garden settings. Plantings of 70,000 azaleas, among the most extensive in the nation, include a number of hybrid groups: Glenn Dale, Kurume, Kaempferi, Ghent, Mollis and Knapp Hill.

The Gotelli Collection of dwarf and slow-growing conifers contains over 1,500 plants covering five acres and representing 30 genera. Naturalistic plantings of ferns and other plants native to eastern North America can be seen in Fern Valley, while Cryptomeria Valley features a collection of Oriental plants. Exhibited in an enclosed pavilion near the Administration Building is a priceless display of 53 bonsai, given to the United States by the Nippon Bonsai Assocation of Japan.

The National Herb Garden covers about two acres and is divided into three sections: the Knot Garden, the historic Rose Garden and the Specialty Gardens. The three-acre National Country Garden displays 13 small gardens appropriate for city dwellers. Also of interest are the 24 sandstone capitol columns, in a setting designed by the late Russell Page, the well-known British landscape artist.

In 1927 Congress approved a bill directing the Secretary of Agriculture to establish an arboretum. The first major planting was installed in 1947-48. The historical significance of the Arboretum was recognized in 1973, when it was placed on the National Register of Historic Places.

Florida

Cypress Gardens

Public Relations Dept.	(800) 282-2123
P.O. Box 1	Nationwide
Cypress Gardens,	(800) 237-4826
FL 33880	in Florida

Hours: every day 8–sunset.
Admission: fee charged.

Directions: 45 miles southwest of Sea World on St. Rd. 540 east, midway between Tampa and Orlando.

Cypress Gardens opened in 1936 on 16 acres of reclaimed swampland. The Gardens have grown to 223 acres and feature tropical and subtropical foliage, a waterskiing show, a zoological park and a swimming and high-diving water spectacular. Over 8,000 varieties of plants (70 percent subtropical and 30 percent tropical) are represented.

The botanical gardens are divided into two main areas: the Original Gardens, the 16-acre tract opened to the public in 1936, and Gardens of the World, offering floral and architectural salutes to foreign countries.

Thomas Edison Winter Home and Botanical Gardens, Fort Myers, Florida.

Thomas Edison Winter Home and Botanical Gardens

2350 McGregor Boulevard   **(813) 334-3614**
Fort Myers, FL 33901

Hours: Mon.–Sat. 9–4; Sun. 12:30–4; closed Dec. 25 and Thanksgiving Day.
Admission: fee charged.
Directions: within 1 mi. of downtown Fort Myers; follow directional signs to Edison Estate, leading from U.S. 41.
Public Transportation: accessible by Leetran Bus System.

The Edison Winter Home is a historic estate where the inventor's chemical laboratory, personal residence, botanical gardens and a memorabilia museum can be toured. The 14 acres of subtropical gardens and vintage buildings are maintained by the City of Fort Myers.

Thomas Edison (1847–1931) imported plants from all over the world and grew them at his southern home—not for their beauty, but for the products and by-products they were capable of yielding. Today, the Gardens contain over 1,000 species of plants experimented on by Edison. The cycads, palms and collection of Ficus Family plants are notable attractions.

In 1947 Mina Edison willed the estate to the City of Fort Myers, to be maintained in remembrance of her husband. The museum was completed in 1970.

Preston B. Bird and Mary Heinlein Fruit and Spice Park

24801 S.W. 187 Avenue   **(305) 247-5727**
Homestead, FL 33031

Hours: every day 10–5; scheduled tour times: Sun. 1 and 3.
Admission: no fee.
Directions: located on Coconut Palm Dr. and Redland Rd. north of Homestead; take U.S. 1 to Princeton, turn west on Coconut Palm Dr. (248 St.); 5 mi. straight ahead to the Park.

Bok Tower Gardens

P.O. Drawer 3810   **(813) 676-1408**
Lake Wales, FL 33859-3810

Hours: every day 8–5:30.
Admission: fee charged.
Directions: near Lake Wales, 40 mi. from Orlando; signs on U.S. 27 and U.S. 60 direct visitors.

Edward Bok acquired land near Lake Wales in 1922 and dreamed of creating "a spot which would reach out its beauty to the people." Frederick Law Olmsted, Jr. was hired to help realize the dream and architect Milton B. Medary was engaged to design a carillon tower. President Calvin Coolidge formally dedicated the grounds and tower in 1929 as a gift from Bok to the American people.

About half of the Gardens' 130 acres are landscaped, with wide curving paths (bordered by ground covers), open vistas and plantings of azaleas, camellias, gardenias and magnolias against a background of ferns, live oaks, pines and a variety of palms. Over 300 kinds of cultivated plants are incorporated into the landscape.

Mirrored in the Reflection Pool is the focal point of the Gardens, the carillon Singing Tower. It is made of pink marble and coquina stone, soars 205 feet and houses 53 bronze bells which fill the Gardens with music daily. The tower is surrounded by a moat in which a variety of water plants, including iris and papyrus, is grown.

Bok Tower Gardens is managed by The American Foundation, a not-for-profit organization established by Bok in 1925.

Fairchild Tropical Garden

10901 Old Cutler Road   **(305) 667-1651**
Miami, FL 33156

Hours: every day 9:30–4:30, except Dec. 25.
Admission: fee charged.
Directions: about 10 mi. southwest of downtown Miami on Old Cutler Rd.
Public Transportation: accessible by bus from Coral Gables.

Fairchild Tropical Garden, the largest tropical botanical garden in the continental U.S., is best known as an attractively landscaped display garden, but it also houses research facilities for studying tropical plants. The 83-acre Garden features about 5,000 different kinds of plants situated among eight lakes, winding paths and open vistas. It is owned and oper-

ated in association with the Metropolitan Dade County Park and Recreation Department.

The palm and cycad collections at Fairchild are among the world's finest and largest. Bromeliads, aroids, orchids, ferns and tropical flowering trees make up other outstanding collections. Plants native to the Everglades, the Florida Keys and the Bahamas are grown in areas simulating their natural habitats.

Originally organized to be a public facility, the Garden officially opened in 1938. It was the creation of Colonel Robert H. Montgomery, a federal tax authority and accountant whose hobby was plants. William Lyman Phillips designed the Garden and it is named after Dr. David Fairchild, the famous plant explorer who was a close friend and advisor to Col. Montgomery.

Vizcaya Museum and Gardens

3251 South Miami Avenue   **(305) 579-2708**
Miami, FL 33129   **4626**

Hours: every day 9:30–5, except Dec. 25; ticket window closes at 4:30.
Admission: fee charged.
Directions: 10 mi. south of downtown Miami; signs posted on I–95.
Public Transportation: accessible by bus and Metrorail Rapid Transit.

Vizcaya, an American realization of an Italian-Renaissance villa and gardens, combines elements of Italian architecture, French and Italian garden design, ocean views and tropical vegetation. Industrialist James Deering employed 1,000 workers to build the estate during 1914–16. The house was opened as a decorative arts museum in a garden setting in 1952, after it was acquired by Dade County.

Leu Botanical Gardens

1730 Forest Avenue   **(305) 894-6021**
Orlando, FL 32803

Hours: gardens, every day 9–5, except Dec. 25; house, Wed.–Sun. 10–4.
Admission: fee charged.
Directions: four mi. northeast of downtown Orlando, just off Hwy. 17 and 92; four blocks off Mills Ave. at Nebraska and Forest.
Public Transportation: accessible by bus.

The Four Arts Garden

Four Arts Plaza   (305) 655-2766
Palm Beach, FL 33480

Hours: year-round, Mon.–Fri. 10–5; Nov.– Apr., Sat. 10–5; Jan. to mid-Apr., Sun. 2:30–5.

View from House to south, Vizcaya Museum and Gardens, Miami, Florida (photo: Doris Littlefield)

Admission: no fee.
Directions: cross the bridge from Okeechobee Blvd. into Palm Beach and onto Royal Palm Way; take the first left into Four Arts Plaza; garden is on the east side of plaza next to the library.

Marie Selby Botanical Gardens

800 S. Palm Avenue   (813) 366-5730
Sarasota, FL 33577

Hours: every day 10–5, except Dec. 25.
Admission: fee charged.
Directions: on the waterfront in downtown Sarasota; Mound St. (Rt. 41) and S. Palm Ave.

At the Marie Selby Botanical Gardens, situated on a peninsula bordered by the Sarasota Bay and the Hudson Bayou, visitors can enjoy the waterfront and more than 10,000 different kinds of plants, including many epiphytes. A highlight is the display greenhouse (7,000 sq. ft.) containing a jungle of orchids, bromeliads, other epiphytes from tropical forests and hanging baskets of gesneriads. Further features include tropical food plants, hibiscus, the Cactus and Succulent Garden, the Herb Garden, a bamboo grove, banyan trees, a lily pond and waterfall, and a trellis area in front of the greenhouse with tropical vines and State-Champion *Ficus* species.

The Selby House, located at the center of the Gardens, became the winter home of Bill and Marie Selby in the 1920s. In 1972 Marie Selby bequeathed her home, gardens and a trust for the development of a botanical garden. The Gardens opened to the public in 1975.

Alfred B. Maclay State Gardens

3540 Thomasville Road   (904) 893-4232
Tallahassee, FL 32308

Hours: park, every day 9–5; Gardens, winter to spring blooming season (Jan.–Apr.)
Admission: fee charged.
Directions: 5½ mi. north of Tallahassee and ¾ mi. north of I–10 on U.S. Hwy. 319 (Thomasville Rd.).

Busch Gardens

3000 Tampa Boulevard   (813) 971-8282
Tampa, FL 33612

Hours: every day 9:30–6; summer and selected holidays 9:30–10.
Admission: fee charged.
Directions: 8 mi. northeast of downtown Tampa and 2 mi. east of I–75 and the Busch Blvd. interchange.

Busch Gardens is a 300-acre African-theme park, and many of the 3,000 animals displayed roam in naturalistic areas landscaped with appropriate plants.

Busch Gardens opened in 1959 on 15 acres of sandy waste land next to Anheuser-Busch's Tampa brewery. It attracts three million visitors annually.

Museum of Botany and the Arts, Marie Selby Botanical Gardens, Sarasota, Florida (photo: Bob Wands)

Georgia

The State Botanical Garden of Georgia

2450 South Milledge Avenue
Athens, GA 30605

Hours: every day 8–8; Visitor Center/Conservatory, every day 9–4:30, except Dec. 25; Callaway Building, every day 8–5.
Admission: no fee.
Directions: on South Milledge Ave., 1 mi. south of the Athens bypass southern terminus; from I–95 take U.S. 441 south to Athens; follow the bypass to South Milledge Ave.

On 293 acres The State Botanical Garden of Georgia aims to conserve rare and unusual

Piedmont species, identify useful landscape plants through display and collect taxonomic plant groups.

Native species are featured along the one-mile scenic Oconee River frontage, in the large flood plain, in the upland forests and in dramatic spring-fed, gorgelike ravines of the Garden. Cultivated sections include the rose garden, one-acre annual and perennial garden, wildflower garden and azalea-camellia garden. Viburnums, dogwoods, redbuds, magnolias and mountain laurels form other flowering displays. The Visitor Center/Conservatory complex, covering ½ acre, was completed in 1985. It houses a reception center, offices and 10,000 sq.-ft. conservatory.

Development of the Garden started in 1968 when the Plant Science faculty proposed the project. By 1972, the Garden's boundaries were established and the Friends of the University of Georgia Botanical Garden, Inc., was formed.

Atlanta Botanical Garden

P.O. Box 77246   (404) 876-5858
Atlanta, GA 30357

Hours: Mon.–Sat. 9–5; Sun. 12–5; Apr.–Oct. 9–8; closed Jan. 1, Dec. 25, Thanksgiving Day, July 4, Labor Day.
Admission: fee charged.
Directions: I–75/85, 14th St. exit, east to dead end at Piedmont Rd.; left three blocks to Prado Entrance into park; follow signs.
Public Transportation: accessible by MARTA bus.

This eight-year-old, 60-acre Botanical Garden in Piedmont Park includes six acres of Japanese, rose, herb, fruit and vegetable, annual and perennial, wildflower-research and native gardens. A newly built attraction, "Gardenhouse," opened in 1985 and the Conservatory under construction is scheduled to open in 1989.

Fernbank Science Center
Fernbank Greenhouse and Botanical Gardens

156 Heaton Park Dr. NE   (404) 378-4311
(Science Center)
765 Clifton Rd. NE
(Greenhouse and
Bot. Gardens)
Atlanta, GA 30307

Hours: Gardens, Mon.–Fri. 8:30–5; Sun. 1–5; Greenhouse, Sun. only 1–5; both closed major holidays.
Admission: no fee for Gardens.
Public Transportation: accessible by MARTA bus.

The Fernbank Science Center uniquely combines a museum, woodland and gardens to "promote an understanding of the upward spirals of science and technology; and to communicate...the harmony and order of the natural world."

The Botanical Gardens have over 1,200 kinds of indigenous and exotic plants. Herbs, annuals, vegetables and bulbs are displayed in the trial display gardens. Roses are grown in the Official Test Garden. The Fernbank Forest represents an undisturbed example of the area's original vegetation. Greenhouses are tropical plant preserves.

The Fernbank Science Center was established in 1966 and is operated by the Dekalb County School System and Fernbank, Inc.

American Camellia Society Headquarters
Massee Lane Camellia Garden

P.O. Box 1217   (912) 967-2358
Fort Valley, GA 31030

Hours: building, Mon.–Fri. 9–4; weekends by appointment; Garden open every day.
Admission: donation accepted.
Directions: 5½ mi. south of Fort Valley on Rt. 49.

Twelve acres of gardens known as Massee Lane Camellia Garden surround the 18th-

Callaway Gardens, Pine Mountain, Georgia

century-style Headquarters building of the American Camellia Society. The structure houses the most extensive camellia library in existence.

Mr. D.C. Strother, the original owner and builder of Massee Lane Garden, donated his camellia garden, farm acreage and money to the American Camellia Society in 1965. He had started planting camellias in the 1930s.

Azaleas, pines, magnolias, crape myrtles and daylilies join the camellias in formal and informal settings. A large display greenhouse contains exotic plants and over 150 varieties of camellias.

Callaway Gardens

Pine Mountain, GA 31822   (404) 663-2281

Hours: winter months, every day 8–5; summer months, 7–6.
Admission: fee charged.
Directions: located about 75 mi. southwest of Atlanta on U.S. Hwy. 27.
Public Transportation: accessible by bus.

Callaway Gardens, adjacent to Pine Mountain Ridge, consists of nearly 14,500 acres (2,500 under intensive development and 4,000 open to the public). The institution was conceived and endowed by Cason J. Callaway, Sr. and his wife, Virginia Hand Callaway, in 1952. Today, the Gardens are owned and operated by the Ida Cason Callaway Foundation.

The Garden's major emphasis is the preservation of native flora. Thirteen miles of paved roads and four major trail systems (Holly, Rhododendron, Azalea and Wildflower) allow visitors access to much of the acreage and intensive plantings. The five-mile Scenic Drive circles Mountain Creek Lake and connects the following: the Azalea Area (about 20 acres), displaying over 600 species and varieties; the Native Flora Area; the Laurel Springs Area, the most natural and undisturbed portion of the Gardens; the Greenhouse and Flower Garden Area (20,000 sq. ft.), containing seasonal floral displays and special collections; the Meadow Lake Area, with over 475 species and varieties of holly; and Mr. Cason's Vegetable Garden — 7½ acres laid out in a semicircle and demonstrating intensive fruit and vegetable culture on a grand scale.

Another major aspect of Callaway Gardens is the summer recreational area: a water-skiing pavilion, circus area, cottage area and three 18-hole golf courses, all centered around Robin Lake.

Hawaii

Waimea Arboretum and Botanical Garden

Waimea Falls Park   (808) 638-8511
59-864 Kamehameha Highway
Haleiwa, HI 96712

Hours: every day 10–5:30.
Admission: fee charged.
Directions: 35 mi. from Honolulu, on the north shore at Waimea Bay, just past Haleiwa.
Public Transportation: Honolulu City Bus stops near entrance.

In the 1,800-acre nature park of Waimea Falls, named for the 45-foot waterfall, over 30 different botanical collections, set among steep valley walls, form the Arboretum and Botanical Garden. About 5,000 kinds of plants can be seen on the 150 acres open to the public. The emphasis is on threatened tropicals and collections include geographic floras of Guam, Bermuda, the Canary Islands, Malaysia, Central and South America and the Mascarene Islands. Many Hawaiian plants are also preserved. The Arboretum has the "world's finest collection" of gingers and heliconias and extensive displays of spider lilies, erythrina and hibiscus.

Foster Botanic Garden

180 N. Vineyard Boulevard   (808) 533-3406
Honolulu, HI 96817

Hours: every day 9–4, except Dec. 25 Jan. 1.
Admission: fee charged.
Directions: in downtown Honolulu.
Public Transportation: accessible by bus.

Foster Botanic Garden, a 20-acre site, is the headquarters for the Honolulu Botanic Gardens, a development totaling 650 acres. Foster Botanic Garden started in 1855 when Queen Kalama sold the property to William Hillebrand who planted many of the trees that now tower over the Garden. Captain and Mrs. Thomas Foster acquired the site in 1867 and continued its development until 1930 when they bequeathed 5½ acres to the City of Honolulu as a public botanical garden. Today, 10,000 native and imported plants are displayed on the expanded site. Palms, orchids (10,000 hybrids), aroids, cycads, heliconias, bromeliads and economic plants are highlights of the collections.

Other gardens in the Honolulu Botanic Garden System:

Wahiawa Garden (1396 California Ave., Wahiawa, 96786):
The cool, humid climate of this site offers displays of tree ferns, palms, anthuriums, aroids, philodendrons, aralias and other tropical species. The 27-acre wooded gulch was used by the Hawaiian Sugar Planters' Association for forestry experiments and as a nursery in the 1920s. In 1950 it was turned over to the City for use as a public garden.

Koko Crater Botanic Garden:
At the eastern end of Oahu, this 200-acre site features dry-land plants.

Ho'omaluhia Botanic Garden:
This 400-acre, high-rainfall site at the foot of the Kane'ohe pali opened to the public in 1982.

Waimea Arboretum and Botanical Garden, Halweia, Hawaii (photo: Nicki Clancey)

Lyon Arboretum, a unit of the University of Hawaii at Manoa, contains 8,500 plant accessions on 124 acres (10 open to the public).

Among featured collections are the Hawaiian Ethnobotanical, Taro Cultivar and Economic Plant. The Arboretum includes outstanding displays of exotic tropicals and plants endemic to Hawaii in natural and landscaped areas. The successive elevations, from 350 to 1,600 feet, provide visitors with fascinating vistas and examples of varying microclimates.

The site was first developed as a Sugar Planters' Experiment Station in 1918.

Harold L. Lyon Arboretum

University of Hawaii	(808) 988-3177
3860 Manoa Road	
Honolulu, HI 86822	

Hours: Mon.–Fri. 9–3, except on state and federal holidays.
Admission: no fee.
Directions: at the end of Manoa Rd.
Public Transportation: accessible by City Bus #5.

Olu Pua Botanical Garden and Plantation

Box 518	(808) 332-8182
Kalaheo, Kauai, HI 96741	

Hours: Mon., Wed. and Fri. 9–1:45.
Admission: fee charged.
Directions: located just past Kalaheo, in the direction of Waimea Canyon on Hwy. 50.

A collection of over 4,000 native and introduced tropical and subtropical fruits, flowers and trees occupies the 12 acres of Olu Pua Garden.

Sections include: the Palm Garden; the Jungle, where paths are darkened with swamp mahogany and other tropical trees laden with bromeliads, anthuriums and vanilla orchids; and the Kua Kua (food) Garden, where visitors may picnic amid tropical herbs and fruit trees. Various parts of the Garden are devoted to plants native to Kauai, and a highlight of the facility is its display of hibiscus hybrids.

The grounds were once part of the estate for the plantation manager of the Kauai Pineapple Company. Still privately owned, the Garden opened to the public in 1968.

Illinois

Garfield Park Conservatory

300 N. Central Park Blvd. (312) 533-1281
Chicago, IL 60624

Hours: every day 9–5; during major
shows, Mon.–Thurs. 10–6, Fri. 9–9.
Admission: no fee.
Directions: in Chicago, ½ block north of
Lake St. on North Central Park Blvd.;
3600 West and 300 North.
Public Transportation: Chicago Transit
Authority buses and L Train stop nearby.

The Garfield Park Conservatory consists of
4,800 types of plants on 4½ acres under glass.
The outstanding collections, displayed in
naturalistic settings within massive conservatory rooms, include Palms, Ferns and Cycads
(some over 100 years old), Cacti and Succulents, Aroids (Arum Family) and Economic
Plants. While these displays are permanent,
two Conservatory rooms are reserved for seasonal shows.

The first glass house was built in 1893 and
more facilities were added later.

Lincoln Park Conservatory

Stockton Drive and (312) 294-4770
Fullerton Parkway
Chicago, IL 60614

Hours: every day 9–5; during major shows,
10–6, Fri. 9–9.
Admission: no fee.
Directions: Lake Shore Dr. to Fullerton
Pkwy.; one block west to Conservatory.
Public Transportation: CTA Routes: 151
Sheridan, 156 LaSalle, 22 Clark, 36 Broad-
way, 73 Armitage.

Erected during 1891-2, Lincoln Park Conservatory is an impressive Victorian installation,
consisting of four glass buildings, 18 propagation houses, cold frames and hotbeds, covering three acres in all. The four conservatories
are the Palm House, Fernery, Tropical House

and Show House where four major displays
are mounted annually. Outdoors, two flower
gardens offer annuals and perennials.

Ladd Arboretum

2024 McCormick Boulevard (312) 864-5181
Evanston, IL 60201

Hours: grounds, every day dawn-dusk;
Ecology Center and solar greenhouse
complex, Tues.–Sat. 9–4:30.
Admission: no fee.
Directions: three mi. north of Chicago;
McCormick Blvd. can be reached from the
Edens Expwy. (I-94) by taking the Demp-
ster St. exit and traveling east.

Ladd Arboretum, on the banks of the North
Shore Channel, is a 23-acre landscaped strip
with trees and shrubs arranged according to
their plant families (Birch, Legume, Maple, Oak
and Pine). Gardens include the Meadow, Prairie Restoration, Cherry Tree Walk, Nut Tree,
Rotary International Friendship (with All-
America Selections roses), Women's Terrace,
Gazebo and Bird Sanctuary. At the hub of the
installation is the Ecology Center, with a passive solar greenhouse (985 sq. ft.) attached.

Developed by means of private funding, the
Arboretum officially opened to the public in
1960.

Chicago Botanic Garden

Lake Cook Road (312) 835-5440
P.O. Box 400
Glencoe, IL 60022

Hours: grounds, every day 8:30–sunset.
Admission: no fee; parking fee charged.
Directions: about 22 mi. north of Chicago
Loop on Edens Expwy. (I-94); exit Lake
Cook Rd. East; Garden is ¼ mi. from
Edens Expwy.

The Chicago Botanic Garden, built on a marshy flood plain, is now a series of islands, lakes and waterways — a 300-acre site with 2,300 kinds of plants.

The main island hosts the Rose Garden (100 varieties) and the Linnaeus Heritage Garden which demonstrates the systematic classification of plants. The Fruit and Vegetable Island displays new varieties in various demonstration gardens. At the east end of the facility, a group of three islands form Sansho-en, a Japanese-style landscape with a dry garden, moss garden and viewing pavilions. At the south end of the Garden, are the Home Landscaping Center (with small gardens appropriate for patios), the Children's Vegetable Gardens and the Learning Garden for the Disabled. Across the water lies a prairie planting. Native plants can be seen in Trees of Illinois, containing 110 species, and in Turnbull Woods, 15 undisturbed acres.

At the hub of the largest island is the Educational Center, completed in 1976. Attached to this facility are ten greenhouses (9,000 sq. ft.) containing cacti, succulent, orchid, fern, gesneriad and other tropical-plant displays. Outside the building is the Trial and Display Garden where more than 10,000 annuals (200 varieties) are grown.

The Chicago Horticultural Society was formed in 1890, and it began building the Chicago Botanical Garden in 1965.

Morton Arboretum was founded as an outdoor museum, with plants arranged conveniently for study. The collection includes nearly 4,000 types of specimens.

The Arboretum is organized according to landscape, geographic, habitat and botanical groups. Landscape displays, subdivided according to function, include: The Hedge Garden, with sheared hedges of over 100 kinds of trees and shrubs; the Tree Evaluation Plot, containing 83 kinds of trees, with five of each type arranged in rows to show how they might appear as street plantings; the Ground Cover Garden, containing woody plants, herbaceous perennials and annuals; the Colored Foliage Collection; the Shrub Collection (35 acres); the Dwarf Beds; and Columnar Trees.

The geographic groups include the Korean, Balkan (Southeast Europe), Caucasian (Central and West Asia), Central European Forest, Chinese and Japanese. American geographic groups being developed comprise Eastern U.S., Wetlands, Appalachian, Native Woody Plants of Northern Illinois, Pacific Northwest, Rocky Mountains, Plains, Southwest and the Ozarks.

There are also two special habitat groups: the Sand Beds, with sand as topsoil, and the Cool Garden, located below a pond and dam installed with plants intolerant of drought.

Joy Morton (1855-1934), founder of Morton Salt Company, started the Arboretum in 1922 on the grounds of his estate.

Morton Arboretum

Route 53 (312) 968-0074
Lisle, IL 60532

Hours: every day, weather permitting; standard-time period, 9–5; daylight-saving-time period, 9–7; Visitor Center, Apr.–Nov., Mon.–Sat. 9:30–5, Sun. 12–5; Dec.–Mar.; Mon.–Sat. 9:30–4, Sun. 12–4.
Admission: fee charged.
Directions: 25 mi. west of downtown Chicago; just north of East-West Tollway (St. Hwy. 5) on Rt. 53.
Public Transportation: accessible by RTA trains to Lisle and Glen Ellyn.

The Oak Park Conservatory

Parks and Recreation (312) 386-4700
Department of Oak Park
1 Village Hall Plaza
Oak Park, IL 60302

Hours: Mon. 2–4, Tues.–Sun. 10–4; closed Thanksgiving Day and Dec. 25.
Admission: no fee.
Directions: located 10 mi. west of the Chicago Loop, on Garfield St. between the Harlem-Ave. and Austin-Blvd. exits of I-290.

Glen Oak Botanical Garden

Peoria Park District   (309) 685-4321
2218 N. Prospect Road
Peoria, IL 61603

Hours: grounds, every day dawn–dusk;
conservatory, every day 8–4.
Admission: no fee.
Directions: I–74 to Peoria; Knoxville Ave.
exit to McClure Ave., turn right and con-
tinue to main entrance of Glen Oak Park;
Garden at intersection of Prospect Rd. and
McClure Ave.
Public Transportation: accessible by bus.

Washington Park Botanical Garden

Location address:	Mailing address:
Washington Park	P.O. Box 5052
Fayette and	Springfield, IL 62705
Chatham Rds.	
Springfield, IL 62704	

Hours: Mon.–Fri. 12–4, Sat. and Sun. 12–5.
Admission: donation requested.
Directions: from I–55 take South Grand
exit; South Grand west to Washington
Park; proceed through park, following
signs.
Public Transportation: accessible by city
bus.

*Education Center and greenhouses, Chicago
Botanic Garden, Glencoe, Illinois*

Indiana

Hayes Regional Arboretum

801 Elks Rd.   (317) 962-3745
Richmond, IN 47374

Hours: Apr. 15 to Nov. 31, Tues.–Sat. 8–5, Sun. 1–5; Dec. 1 to Apr. 14, Tues.–Sat. 8–5; closed Mon.
Admission: no fee.
Directions: located 3 mi. west of the Indiana-Ohio border; take U.S. 40 west exit from I–70; travel 2½ mi. to entrance.

Iowa

Bickelhaupt Arboretum

340 South 14th St.   (319) 242-4771
Clinton, IA 52732

Hours: every day dawn–dusk.
Admission: no fee.
Directions: 20 mi. north of the junction of I–80 and Rt. 67; in the center of Clinton.
Public Transportation: accessible by city bus (stop 2 blocks away).

Des Moines Botanical Center

909 East River Dr.   (515) 283-4148
Des Moines, IA 50316

Hours: Mon.–Thurs. 10–6, Fri. 10–9, weekends 10–5; closed Thanksgiving Day, Dec. 25 and Jan 1.
Admission: fee charged.
Directions: located on the east bank of the Des Moines River between the University Ave. bridge and the MacVicar Frwy. (I–235) bridge; from I–235 take the East 6th St. exit.

Kansas

The Bartlett Arboretum

Box 39   (316) 488-3451
Belle Plaine, KS 67013

Hours: Apr. 1 to mid-Nov., every day 9–6.
Admission: fee charged.
Directions: 20 mi. south of Wichita on Hwy. 55.

The Bartlett Arboretum was started in 1910 by Dr. Walter E. Bartlett. The 20-acre tract of wooded gardens represents the "only arboretum of maturity between the Mississippi River and the Rockies." The Arboretum contains trees, shrubs, grasses and flowers from all over the world, that tolerate the Kansas climate. The extensive formal garden includes courtyards, hedge-bordered beds, terraces, sunken areas and fountains.

Gage Park: Reinisch Rose Garden, Doran Rock Garden, Conservatory, Topeka Zoo

4320 W. 10th St.   (913) 232-1484
Topeka, KS 66604

Hours: Rose Garden, every day 6–11; Conservatory, Mon.–Fri. 8–4:30, Sun. 2–4; Zoo, every day 9–5.
Admission: Gardens, no fee; Zoo, fee charged.
Directions: I–70 to Gage Blvd., south to 6th St.; right on 6th; left into Gage Park.
Public Transportation: accessible by bus from downtown.

Kentucky

Bernheim Forest, Arboretum and Nature Center

Clermont, KY 40110   (502) 543-2451

Administration Office, Cave Hill Cemetery
Louisville, Kentucky

Hours: Mar. 15 to Nov. 15, every day 9–sundown; Nature Center Museum closed Mon.
Admission: no fee.
Directions: 30 mi. south of Louisville on State Rd. 245 (2 mi. east of I-65).

Bernheim Forest is a preserve of 10,000 acres, 2,000 of which have been developed for educational and recreational uses. The Arboretum and Nature Center cover 250 acres. The landscaped Arboretum features 1,500 kinds of plants. Specialized collections include crabap-

ples, nut trees, beech, ginkgos, oaks, horse-chestnuts, buckeyes, dogwood, azaleas, viburnums, dwarf conifers and maples. The installation has been designated by the Holly Society of America as an official Holly Arboretum.

Bernheim Forest had its beginnings in 1928 when Mr. Isaac Wolfe Bernheim bought 14,000 acres of land for the purpose of conservation. The facility is owned and operated by the Isaac W. Bernheim Foundation.

Rosedown Plantation and Gardens,
St. Francisville, Louisiana

Lexington Cemetery

883 West Main St.   (606) 255-5522
Lexington, KY 40508

Hours: grounds, every day 8–5; special
holidays until dusk; office, Mon.–Sat. 8–4,
Sun. 1–4.
Admission: no fee.
Directions: about 1 mi. west of courthouse.

Cave Hill Cemetery

701 Baxter Ave.   (502) 451-5630
Louisville, KY 40204   584-8363

Hours: every day 8–4:45.

Admission: no fee.
Directions: 3 mi. from I-64 at the Grinstead
Dr. exit.

Louisiana

Hodges Garden

P.O. Box 900   (318) 586-3523
Many, LA 71449

Hours: Gardens, every day 8–sunset;
greenhouses, spring–summer, every day
9–5; fall–winter 9–4:30; closed Dec. 24
25 and Jan. 1.
Admission: fee charged.
Directions: on Hwy 171, halfway between

Shreveport and Lake Charles; 12 mi. south of Many and opposite Toro Hills Resort.

Hodges Gardens, known as the "garden in the forest," began in the 1940s as a 4,700-acre experimental reforestation project headed by pioneer conservationist A.J. Hodges. A ten-mile drive circles the 225-acre lake at the heart of the Gardens. Points of interest around the lake include the Louisiana Purchase Memorial, natural areas and scenic overlooks, wildlife pastures, Lookout Tower, the conservatory and greenhouses (displaying tropical collections) and 60 acres of formal gardens with extensive plantings of tulips, dogwood and azaleas, annuals and roses. Abandoned stone quarries provide the Gardens with multi-level settings, and water pumped from the lake forms pools, waterfalls and streams.

Hodges Gardens was formally dedicated in 1959 and is owned and operated today by the not-for-profit Hodges Foundation.

Audubon Park and Zoological Garden

6500 Magazine St.   (504) 861-2537
P.O. Box 4327
New Orleans, LA 70178

Hours: Mon.–Fri. 9:30–4:30, weekends 9:30–5:30; closed Thanksgiving Day, Dec. 25, Jan. 1 and Mardi Gras; other holidays 9:30–5:30.
Admission: fee charged.
Directions: from downtown New Orleans, take Magazine St. to Audubon Park.
Public Transportation: accessible by St. Charles streetcar and Broadway bus.

Longue Vue House and Gardens

7 Bamboo Rd.   (504) 488-5488
New Orleans, LA 70124

Hours: Tues.–Fri. 10–4:30, Sat. and Sun. 1–5; closed Mon. and national holidays.

Admission: fee charged.
Directions: off I-10 Expwy. at Metairie-Rd. exit; a short distance from downtown New Orleans.
Public Transportation: accessible by Canal-Metairie Rd. buses.

Longue Vue House and Gardens is an eight-acre city estate built between 1939 and 1942 in the classical tradition. Its Gardens are influence by English and Spanish styles and contain examples of Greek-Revival architecture. The basic plan of the estate is a large formal garden, the Spanish Court, surrounded by a series of smaller plantings, each unique in color scheme and character. Throughout, a total of 25 fountains create a cooling effect and provide a unifying aquatic theme. Oaks, magnolias, camellias, azaleas, roses, sweet-olives, crape myrtles and oleanders are combined with seasonal floral displays.

Longue Vue was designed and built for Mr. and Mrs. Edgar B. Stern. In 1968, the year the estate opened to the public, Mrs. Stern established the Longue Vue Foundation to preserve and maintain the facility.

Rosedown Plantation and Gardens

P.O. Box 1816   (504) 635-3332
St. Francisville, LA 70775

Hours: Mar.–Oct., every day 9–5; Nov.–Feb., 10–4; closed Dec. 24 and 25.
Admission: fee charged.
Directions: 25 mi. north of Baton Rouge, via U.S. 61 or La. Hwy. 10.

Rosedown, a restored Southern manor (mansion and Gardens) with 2,400 acres of surrounding land, functions as an example of plantation life as it was before the Civil War. The mansion and 30-acre Gardens were begun in 1835, and many plants dte back to that time.

The avenue leading to the mansion is shaded by live oaks nearly 200 years old. Closer to the structure are both formal and utilitarian gardens: the Flower Garden, North Parterre, Eve's Garden, Herb Garden and Medicinal Herb Garden. Throughout the grounds, plants have grown to maturity and express their natural character. The grove of century-old camellias, for example, is 25 feet tall. Mature azaleas, crape myrtles, sweet-olives and conifers are other featured plants. Sixteen rooms of the two-story mansion may be toured.

In 1956 Catherine Underwood of Houston, Texas, visited Rosedown just as the estate had been put on the market. Impressed with the original beauty of the gardens, she and her husband decided to buy the property, embarking on an eight-year restoration progrm. Catherine opened Rosedown to the public in 1964. Since her death in 1970, her family has continued to operate the site, now a division of Feliciana Corporation.

Japanese Teahouse, Brookside Gardens, Wheaton, Maryland

Maryland

William Paca House and Garden

1 Martin St.	(301) 269-0601
Annapolis, MD 21401	267-6656

Hours: Garden, Mon.–Sat. 10–4; Sun., Nov.–Apr., noon–4; May–Oct., noon–5; closed Thanksgiving Day and Dec. 25; House, Tues.–Sat., 10–4, Sun. and holidays noon–4; closed Mon., Thanksgiving Day and Dec. 25.
Admission: fee charged.
Directions: Take Rowe-Blvd. exit from U.S. 50, left from Rowe onto College Ave., right on King George St.; entrance on Martin St.

William Paca, a signer of the Declaration of Independence and an early governor of Maryland, built his house and garden between 1765 and 1772. By 1900 the sadly neglected garden had been completely covered by a hotel, parking lot and bus depot.

When Paca's historic house was threatened in 1965, Historic Annapolis, Inc., a preservation group, acted to save the structure. Further efforts by the group led to the complete restoration of the colonial garden based on archaeological findings and evidence from paintings.

Today, the terraced and walled town Garden includes many native plants admired in the 18th century, heirloom garden perennials and old varieties of roses.

London Town Publik House and Gardens

839 Londontown Rd.	(301) 956-4900
Edgewater, MD 21037	

Hours: Tues.–Sat. 10–4; Sun. 12–4, closed Mon., Dec. 25, Thanksgiving Day, Jan. and Feb.
Admission: fee charged.
Directions: 7 mi. from Annapolis; take Rt. 2 south to Lee Airport in Edgewater; turn left onto Mayo Rd. (Rt. 253) and proceed 1 mi., turn left onto Londontown Rd.

London Town Publik House and Gardens is a National Historic Landmark maintained by the Department of Recreation and Parks. The Publik House, dating to the middle of the 18th century, is the only remaining structure on the site of a once-thriving seaport town.

Eleven acres adjoining the Publik House and fronting South River feature native trees, shrubs and wildflowers. Along the winding paths, magnolias, hollies, cherries, viburnums, conifers, peonies and Japanese iris are displayed. The Gardens also serve as a testing facility for winter-hardy camellias. Specialty areas include the Winter Garden and Salt Marsh Walk. Near the Publik House, herbs and 18th-century crops are grown.

Garden development began in 1970, and the site opened to the public in 1972.

Ladew Topiary Gardens

3535 Jarrettsville Pike   (301) 557-9466
Monkton, MD 21111

Hours: Gardens, mid–Apr. to Oct., Tues.– Fri. 10–4, Sat.–Sun. noon–5; Manor House, Wed., Sat., Sun. during garden hours or by special arrangement otherwise; open year-round for group tours by appointment.
Admission: fee charged.
Directions: on Rt. 146, 14 mi. north of I–695 (Baltimore Beltway) exit 27 north.

The House and Gardens of Ladew were developed as a private estate between 1929 and 1976. Harry S. Ladew restored and enlarged an old house (late 1700s) and furnished it with a mixture of styles. On 22 acres outdoors, he designed and developed 15 secluded gardens (surrounding a central bowl, terraces and allee) that are outlined by a third of a mile of tall sculptured hedges.

The topiary figures Ladew Gardens is famous for depict a huntsman and hounds chasing a fox, swans floating on undulating waves of yew, seahorses, lyre birds, a unicorn, giraffe, top hat, heart and arrow, Churchill's "V for Victory," a Chinese junk and a Buddha.

In creating his gardens, Ladew focused on specific themes. There are pink, yellow, red and white gardens, each filled with flowering

plants that carry the color from spring through summer. Others include the Wild Garden, Victorian Garden, Berry Garden, Rose Garden, Garden of Eden (an apple orchard underplanted with azaleas, complete with a statue of Adam and Eve) Waterlily Garden, Iris Garden, Terrace Garden, Herb Garden (30 varieties of herbs) and Portico Garden.

Before Mr. Ladew died in 1976, he set up a foundation to run the Gardens and house. Both are in the National Register of Historic Places.

Brookside Gardens

1500 Glenallan Ave.   (301) 949-8230
Wheaton, MD 20902

Hours: conservatories, every day 9–5; grounds, every day 9–sunset; closed Dec. 25.
Admission: no fee.
Directions: 10 mi. north of Washington, D.C.; from Beltway (495) take exit 31A (Rt. 97) north towards Wheaton; continue for 3 mi. to Randolph Rd. and turn right; right again at Glenallan Ave.; continue 3/4 mi.; Gardens are on the right.
Public Transportation: 10–minute walk from bus stop.

Established in 1969, Brookside Gardens, a 50-acre display garden, is operated by the Maryland National Capitol Park and Planning Commission.

A series of small gardens are connected by walkways and waterways. The Formal Gardens, three connected courtyards terraced on a hillside, feature perennials, annuals and flowering plum trees set off by fountains. In the Rose Garden over 600 plants (40 varieties) are grouped with evergreens, ornamental grasses and ground covers. In the Trial Garden, unusual plants and designs provide innovative ideas for the home gardener. Other areas include the Fragrance Garden, Viburnum Garden, Winter Garden, Azalea and Woodland Garden (7½ acres) Aquatic Garden and the Gude Garden where a Japanese-style pavilion overlooks a lake and rolling hills. Conservatories cover 8,400 sq. ft. and feature year-round floral displays.

Massachusetts

Isabella Stewart Gardner Museum

2 Palace Rd.	(617) 566-1401
Boston, MA 02115	

Hours: Tues. 12–9 (July to Aug., 12–5); Wed.–Sun. 12–5; closed Mon. and national holidays.
Admission: fee charged.
Directions: from Mass. Tpk. take exit 22; Rt. 9 (Huntington Ave.) past Museum of Fine Arts to Longwood Ave.; right on Longwood, then right on Palace Rd.
Public Transportation: Museum–Ruggles stop by bus or train.

The Gardner Museum is the achievement of Isabella Stewart Gardner (1860–1924) who designed the building and endowed it to house her personal collection of about 2,000 art objects. Fenway Court, an indoor courtyard filled with plants, was designed in the style of a 15th-century Venetian palace.

Mount Auburn Cemetery

580 Mount Auburn St.	(617) 547-7105
Cambridge, MA 02138	

Hours: grounds, May 1 to Oct. 1, every day 8–7; rest of the year 8–5; office closed Sun. and holidays.
Admission: no fee.
Directions: on Rt. 16 at the Cambridge-Watertown boundary line.
Public Transportation: accessible by MTA.

Mount Auburn Cemetery, the first garden cemetery in America, has about 2,500 identified trees on its 170 acres. Over 350 different varieties are represented; many are over 100 years old with trunks exceeding three feet in diameter. Hilly terrain and three lakes add to the beauty of the grounds. In addition to the extensive tree collection, there are over 40,000 annual plants, 5,000 to 10,000 bulbs, beds of perennials and thousands of shrubs.

Started in 1831 by Dr. Jacob Bigelow and the Massachusetts Horticultural Society, the Cemetery/garden is owned by the Proprietors of the Cemetery of Mount Auburn.

Garden in the Woods of the New England Wild Flower Society

Hemenway Road	(617) 877-6574
Framingham, MA 01701	

Hours: Apr. 15 through Oct., Tues–Sun. 9–4.
Admission: fee charged.
Directions: Rt. 128 to Rt. 20 west; 7½ mi. to Raymond Rd.; 1.3 mi. to Hemenway Rd.

Garden in the Woods consists of 45 acres of rolling hills, woodlands, ponds, brooks, trails and wildflowers, and includes the largest (15 acres) landscaped collection of northeastern native plants (1,500 species and varieties). The Garden is owned and operated by the New England Wild Flower Society (NEWFS) whose purpose is education and research in native-plant conservation, botany, ecology and horticulture.

Trails wind through a number of specialty gardens: Western, Meadow, Sunny Bog, Lily Pond, Lady's-Slipper Path and Rich-Woodland Groves. Also featured is a 1,000-sq.–ft. solar greenhouse.

W.C. Curtis and H. Stiles began the subtle landscaping in the 1930s, but it continues to be developed and refined by NEWFS.

The Arnold Arboretum, Jamaica Plain, Massachusetts (photo: C. Lobig)

The Arnold Arboretum

Jamaica Plain, MA 02130   **(617) 524-1718**
524-1717
(recorded info.)

Hours: every day, sunrise–sunset.
Admission: no fee; donations accepted.
Directions: located on the Arborway, 12 mi. south of downtown Boston, near the junction of Rts. 1 and 230.
Public Transportation: accessible by Forest Hills Subway (Orange Line) or the Arborway car or bus.

Over 7,000 varieties of ornamental trees and shrubs from all over the North Temperate Zone are planted throughout The Arnold Arboretum. An affiliate of Harvard University and a part of the Boston Park System, it serves the local community as a 265-acre oasis of nature.

The Arboretum is divided into several general areas, each featuring a number of different kinds of plants, many old and noted specimens. One area is devoted to leguminous trees; another features shrubs and vines, from barberries to wisterias. In the meadow, native wildflowers grow among willows and flowering shrubs. Along the Chinese Path are arrangements of Asiatic plants, including many of the original introductions from China. On Hemlock Hill, numerous rhododendrons, azaleas and mountain-laurels are shaded by a canopy of natural woods. Other sizeable and notable collections include lilacs, crabapples, conifers, dwarf conifers, maples and viburnums. Bonsai are displayed in a pavilion near the Dana Greenhouses.

Established in 1872, the Arnold Arboretum is the oldest public arboretum in America, and its history is laced with prominent horticultural figures. Charles Sprague Sargent, the first director of the Arboretum, collaborated with Frederick Law Olmsted in designing the grounds. Most of Olmsted's original plan has been maintained. E.H. "Chinese" Wilson, the famous plant explorer, also served on Arnold's staff.

The Botanic Garden of Smith College

Lyman Plant House   **(413) 584-2700**
Northampton, MA 01063   **ext. 2748**

Hours: grounds, every day at all times; greenhouses, every day 8–4.
Admission: no fee.
Directions: north of Springfield; take exit 19 from I-91; left onto Rt. 9 north and continue through Northampton to College La.; left on College La., one block to greenhouse.

The teaching of botany and horticulture, a part of Smith College since the 1880's, has been facilitated over the years by a series of campus greenhouses and gardens. These now contain over 3,500 kinds of plants.

The Lyman Plant House, a conservatory built in 1896 and expanded a number of times from 1902 to 1981, is a major horticultural attraction. Individual sections include: Warm Temperate House; Stove House, with an aquatic tank, orchids and bromeliads; Cold Storage House, where bulbs and spring flowers are forced each year; Temperate House; Palm House; Fern House; Cold Temperate House; Succulent House; and Show House.

The whole campus, dotted with mature woody plants, serves as an arboretum. The original plan, laid out in 1895 by Frederick Law Olmsted, called for the entire grounds to function as a botanical garden, with plant materials selected and arranged both for aesthetic and scientific purposes. Herbaceous gardens and a rock garden are adjacent to the conservatory. Other areas of interest on the campus are the Capen Gardens, with formal beds of tulips and annuals, and the President's House featuring a terraced rose garden and an herb garden.

Heritage Plantation of Sandwich

Grove St.   (617) 888-3300
Box 566
Sandwich, MA 02563

Hours: mid–May to mid–Oct., every day 10–5.
Admission: fee charged.
Directions: 3 mi. from Cape Cod Sagamore Bridge; Rt. 130 to Pine St. and the Museum.
Public Transportation: train, connecting to shuttle bus.

Seventy-six acres of landscaped grounds, flower beds and nature trails, featuring over 1,000 kinds of trees, shrubs and flowers, surround Heritage Plantation, a museum of diversified Americana. The site was once the property of Charles O. Dexter, known for hybridizing rhododendrons. Horticultural highlights include thousands of Dexter rhododendrons and over 550 varieties of daylilies. The Plantation opened to the public in 1969.

Berkshire Garden Center

Box 826   (413) 298-3926
Stockbridge, MA 10262

Hours: mid-May to mid-Oct., every day 10–5.
Admission: fee charged.
Directions: located on both sides of Rt. 102, 2 mi. west of Stockbridge, just past the intersection of Rts. 102 and 183.
Public Transportation: Berkshire Regional Transit.

With the Berkshire Hills as a backdrop, this 15-acre Garden, started in 1934, features daylilies and other perennials, primroses, conifers and shrubs. In addition to various intimate landscaped areas, highlights include herb, flower and rose gardens, pond area and edible landscape (with herbs and vegetables grown in raised beds). Three kinds of greenhouses may be toured.

Naumkeag

The Choate Estate   (413) 298-3239
Stockbridge, MA 01262

Hours: Sat. of Memorial Day through Mon. of Columbus Day, weekends and Mon. holidays; last Tues. in June through Mon. of Labor Day, everyday except Mondays.
House Tours, 10–4:15
Gardens, 10–5
Admission: fee charged.
Directions: on Prospect Hill off Main St. in Stockbridge.

Old Sturbridge Village

Sturbridge, MA 01566   **(617) 347-3362**

Hours: Apr.–Oct., every day 9–5; Nov.–March 10–4; closed Mon. (during winter), Dec. 25 and Jan 1.
Location: Rt. 20 west in Sturbridge; Mass. Tpke. (Rt. 90), exit 9; I-84, exit 3.
Public Transportation: Peter Pan Bus lines from Springfield and Boston; Amtrak trains from New York and Boston to Worcester.

Old Sturbridge Village is a living-history museum that recreates a New England town of the 1830s. Covering 200 acres and containing 40 restored buildings, the attraction includes people in historical dress demonstrating the life, work and community festivities of 19th-century New Englanders.

Horticultural highlights are the Herb Garden exhibit (300 varieties), door-yard gardens and formal gardens. Kitchen gardens offer early 19th century vegetable varieties, and fruits and field crops typical of the period are also grown.

In 1986 Old Sturbridge Village celebrated its fortieth year as a public attraction.

The Margaret C. Ferguson Greenhouses, Alexandra Botanic Garden, and Hunnewell Arboretum, Wellesley College

Central St.   **(617) 235-0320**
Wellesley, MA 02181   **ext. 3074**

Hours: every day 8:30–4:30.
Admission: no fee.
Directions: greenhouses are behind the Science Center off College Road.

Walter Hunnewell Pinetum

845 Washington St.   **(617) 235-0422**
Wellesley, MA 02181

Hours: Mon.–Sat. 8–6, by appointment only.
Admission: no fee.
Directions: on Rt. 16, between Wellesley and South Natick.

The Walter Hunnewell Pinetum was founded in 1852 by H.H. Hunnewell, and although it is still private, the grounds have always been open to the public. The outstanding features of the 39-acre property include rhododendrons and azaleas, topiaries and a conifer collection offering many mature specimens. Also of interest is an 18-section Victorian conservatory (about half of it in active use) housing an orchid collection.

The Stanley Park of Westfield, Inc.

400 Western Ave.   **(413) 568-9312**
P.O. Box 1191
Westfield, MA 01085

Hours: every day 8–dusk from Mother's Day to Columbus Day. Recreation facility open year-round
Admission: no fee.
Directions: Park entrances on Kensington and Western Aves.
Public Transportation: accessible by bus.

Horticultural attractions in the 200-acre Stanley Park include a formal rose garden, Japanese garden, a five-acre arboretum and a rhododendron display garden. The Park was founded in 1945.

The Case Estates of the Arnold Arboretum

Location:	Mailing Address:
135 Wellesley St.	The Arnold Arboretum
Weston, MA 02193	Jamaica Plain, MA 02130
	(617) 524-1718

Hours: every day 9–sunset.
Admission: no fee.
Directions: 13 mi. from the Arnold Arbore-

tum; from Rt. 20 west take left onto Wellesley St.; from Rt. 90, exit Rt. 30–Weston; take 30 west for 2.5 mi., turn right onto Wellesley St., proceed 1 mi.

The Case Estates, on a 75-acre suburban site, serves as nursery and experimental station for the Arnold Arboretum. Areas of interest include ground-cover plots (140 types), Rhododendron Display Garden, Perennial Garden (emphasizing native-American plants) and collections of hosta, daylilies, iris and peonies.

The Arnold Arboretum was left this property in 1944 by sisters Louisa and Marian Case. The estate had been used for over 30 years by Marian Case as the setting for her school of agriculture and gardening.

Michigan

Matthaei Botanical Garden

University of Michigan   (313) 764-1168
1800 North Dixboro Rd.
Ann Arbor, MI 48105

Hours: grounds, every day sunrise–sunset; Conservatory, 10–4:30; gift shop, the first full weekend of each month; closed Thanksgiving Day, Dec. 25 and Jan. 1.
Admission: fee charged.
Directions: take the Geddes exit off U.S. 23; turn right on Geddes and left on Dixboro; Garden is within 100 yards.

The Matthaei Botanical Garden, encompassing 250 acres, displays a collection of 3,500 kinds of plants. The conservatory, the highlight of the Garden, consists of three houses covering 13,000 sq. ft. Each house encloses a distinct climate, bringing together plants from tropical, temperate and desert areas.

Much of the tract outdoors is maintained as natural habitats: bogs, ponds, streams, flood plain, upland forest and meadow. More than 700 species of native plants can be seen along winding trails. Other naturalistic areas are the Woodland Garden and prairie. Centered

around the Conservatory are the Medicinal and Herb, the Rose and Perennial and the Rhododendron and Heath Gardens.

Cranbrook House and Gardens

380 Lone Pine Rd.   (313) 645-3149
P.O. Box 801
Bloomfield Hills, MI 48013

Hours: May, every day 1–5; June–Aug., Mon.–Sat. 10–5, Sun. 1–5; Sept., every day 1–5; Oct., weekends only, 1–5.
Admission: fee charged.
Directions: from Detroit take Woodward Ave. to Lone Pine Rd.; from the north or Chicago, follow U.S. 24 (Telegraph Rd.) to Lone Pine Rd.

The charm of the early 1900s and the personalities of the Booth family can still be felt at Cranbrook House and Gardens. The Mansion, built in 1908, was designed by the prominent architect Albert Kahn; 40 acres of gardens surround it. The estate is now an adjunct of the Cranbrook Educational Community.

In addition to mature trees, outstanding vistas and rolling hills, a variety of planted areas are offered at Cranbrook: the Greek Theater features stone seats and a turf stage; Pine Hill Cascade, a line of decorative stepped basins, carries water to a series of pools. Cen-

Hidden Lake Gardens, Tipton, Michigan

tered around the House are three landscaped levels: the Library Garden, sporting English sculpture; the Promenade, leading to the Reflecting Pool, and the Bog, a naturalized site. On the North Terraces, flower beds line brick paths and stone walls. Turtle Fountain graces the Circular Terrace.

Anna Scripps Whitcomb Conservatory

Belle Isle Park　　　　(313) 267-7133
Detroit, MI 48207

Hours: every day 9–6
Admission: no fee.
Directions: located 2 mi. east of downtown Detroit on Belle Isle in the Detroit River; take Jefferson Ave. to E. Grand Blvd., across the MacArthur Bridge.
Public Transportation: accessible by bus.

Frederick Law Olmsted created the original master plan for Detroit's Belle Isle Park in 1883. The Whitcomb Conservatory, situated in the city-owned Park, was completed in 1904 and rebuilt in 1955, with its Victorian character maintained. The massive Palm House is filled with towering tropicals that can grow as tall as 85 feet before touching the structure's highest point. Other collections include orchids, southwest-American plants and ferns. Six major flower displays are staged annually in the Show House.

Formal gardens surrounding the Conservatory provide horticultural interest outdoors. These plantings, together with the Victorian glass house, cover about ten acres of the 1,000-acre Park.

W.J. Beal Botanical Garden and MSU Campus

Michigan State University　　(517) 355-0348
East Lansing, MI 48823

Hours: every day dawn-dusk.
Admission: no fee.
Directions: on MSU campus; East Circle Dr.,

off Collingwood Entrance from East Grand River.

The W.J. Beal Botanical Garden, started in 1873, is a five-acre installation with about 5,500 species of plants organized according to economic, systematic, landscape and ecological classifications. On two-and-a-half acres of the 5,200-acre campus are the Horticulture Gardens, displaying All-America Selections annuals (800 species) and roses. In addition, plantings are dispersed throughout the campus, with several genera assembled at specific locations.

Founded in 1855, MSU is recorded as being the nation's first land-grant university and as having the first horticulture department; this was established by the eminent Liberty Hyde Bailey.

Dow Gardens

1018 W. Main St.　　　　(517) 631-2677
Midland, MI 48640

Hours: every day 10–sunset; closed Thanksgiving Day, Dec. 24, 25, 31 and Jan. 1.
Admission: fee charged.
Directions: entrance is on the corner of Eastman Rd. (Business Rt. 10) and W. St. Andrews Rd., about 2 mi. south of U.S. 10; exit on Eastman Rd.; Gardens are adjacent to Midland Center for the Arts.

Dow Gardens, once the estate of Herbert H. Dow, founder of Dow Chemical Company, constitutes 65 acres of landscaped and naturalistic areas. Bulbs, annuals, perennials, wildflowers and over 800 types of woody plants form displays that "exhibit a composition of man with nature."

Notable collections of crabapples, pines, junipers, rhododendrons and other ericaceous plants are interspersed among numerous flower displays. Additional features include: Herb Garden, Native Wildflowers, Perennial Border, Rose Garden, Sensory Trail, All-America Display Garden, Test Bedding Plant Area (300 species and/or cultivars). Punctuating the landscape are statuary, picturesque bridges, streams, waterfalls, pools with aquatic plants, lakes and a display greenhouse (3,000 sq. ft.)

The Gardens were started in 1899 for the enjoyment of friends and associates of the Dow family. Today, the institution is an agency of the Herbert H. and Grace A. Dow Foundation.

Fernwood

1720 Range Line Rd.	**(616) 695-6491**
Niles, MI 49120	**or 6688**

Hours: Mar. 1 to Dec. 15, weekdays 9–5, Sat. 10–5, Sun. 12–5.
Admission: fee charged, except on Mother's Day and during the Fall Harvest Show and Plant Benefit Sales.
Directions: U.S. 31, north of Niles, to Walton Rd.; Walton to Range Line Rd.; U.S. 12 to Buchanan Exit (Redbud Trail); turn right onto River St.; River to Range Line Rd.

Fernwood, an educational center, combines a botanic garden and arboretum, a nature center and an arts and crafts center. On the 105-acre site, over 3,000 kinds of native and exotic plants can be found in natural and landscaped areas.

Five acres of gardens and a greenhouse (1,300 sq. ft.) demonstrate home landscape ideas for the Michigan-Indiana area. In the Rock and Bog Garden, an extensive collection of dwarf conifers is combined with heaths, heathers, primroses, iris, ferns, saxifrages and bulbs. Assembled in the 40-acre arboretum are examples of all of Michigan's native trees, plus trees recommended for street and home use. Eighteen acres of Fernwood's grounds are devoted to nature study (over 100 species of ferns are presented), and five acres form a recreated tall-grass prairie.

Fernwood opened to the public in 1964 when Mrs. Mary L. Plym purchased 16 acres and provided an endowment for the development of an educational preserve.

Hidden Lake Gardens

Michigan State University	**(517) 431-2060**
Tipton, MI 49287	

Hours: grounds, Apr.–Oct., weekdays 8 to 30 min. before sundown; Nov.–Mar., weekdays 8–4:30; weekends and holidays 9–4:30; Garden Center Building, weekdays 8–noon, 12:30–4:30; weekends and holidays 12–6; closed during the winter; conservatory, same hours as the grounds; closes at 7, Apr.–Oct., and at 4:30, Nov.–Mar.
Admission: fee charged; no fee Nov.–Mar.

On 670 acres of knolls and valleys among Michigan's Irish Hills, the grounds and conservatories of Hidden Lake Gardens exhibit about 5,200 plant taxa. Seven miles of roadway and trails radiating from six-acre Hidden Lake allow visitors access to the plantings.

Collections include crabapples, flowering cherries, hawthorns, junipers, lilacs, magnolias, maples, mountain ashes, pines, rhododendrons, azaleas, shrub roses, spruces, dwarf and rare conifers, willows and yews. Featured sections are the Demonstration Garden, Ground Covers, Ornamental Evergreens, Exotic Evergreens, the Great Meadow, Lowland Hardwoods, Aristocrats and Oak Upland Forests. The conservatory complex (8,000 sq. ft.) consists of the Temperate House and two domed structures — the Tropical House and the Arid House.

Mr. Harry Fee, a prominent local businessman, started the Gardens in 1926; he gave them to Michigan State University in 1945.

Minnesota

Minnesota Landscape Arboretum and Horticultural Research Center

University of Minnesota	**(612) 443-2460**
3675 Arboretum Dr.	
P.O. Box 39	
Chanhassen, MN 55317	

Hours: Closed major holidays; call ahead for specifics; otherwise, grounds: summer—every day, 8–dusk; winter—every day 8–5:30; buildings: weekdays—8–4:30; weekends—11–4:30
Admission: fee charged; no fee for members.
Directions: Minnesota St. Hwy. 5, 9 mi. west of I–94.

Rolling hills (with natural stands of maple, linden, ash, oak and hornbeam), open fields, two natural lakes, marshland and landscape gardens can all be found on the 550 acres of the Minnesota Landscape Arboretum open to the public (total acres number 975). Three miles of roads and more than six miles of walking trails facilitate exploration of the various areas. Extensive plant collections and demonstration gardens offer new ideas to homeowners, and research conducted at the site focuses on woody ornamentals and fruit trees and their adaptation to northern climates.

The Arboretum's original 160 acres were purchased by the Minnesota State Horticultural Society and donated to the University in 1958. The Arboretum Foundation was established in 1970, and the Arboretum and Horticultural Research Center were administratively combined in 1984.

Como Park Conservatory

Midway Pkwy. and (612) 489-1740
Kaufman Dr.
St. Paul, MN 55103

Hours: every day 10–6.
Admission: fee charged; no fee mid–Apr. to mid–Nov.
Directions: 2 mi. north I–94, just west of Lexington Ave.
Public Transportation: accessible by bus.

The Como Park Conservatory, covering about three acres, was planned in 1913 by the Board of Park Commissioners and completed in 1915.

Today, the display houses contain many of their original plantings. About 200 taxa are represented, with over 200 permanently planted specimens and seasonal floral displays. The Central Palm House (100 ft. in diameter, 65 ft. tall) shelters 26 species of palms. Economic plants, plants mentioned in the Bible, Flower Shows, Sunken Gardens, ferns and cacti are featured in other houses. Just outside the Conservatory are the McKnight Formal Gardens. The Japanese Garden is another of the Park's horticultural features.

Mississippi

The Crosby Arboretum

3702 Hardy St. (601) 264-5249
Hattiesburg, MS 39401

Hours: by appointment.
Admission: no fee.
Directions: adjacent to the State Hospitality Center on I–59, Picayune, MS.

The Crosby Arboretum is a living tribute to L.O. Crosby, Jr., with a permanent collection and display of native trees and plants for purposes of education and research. L.O. Crosby, Jr. (1907–1978), whose father founded the Goodyear Yellow Pine Company, was involved in horticultural endeavors much of his life. His family established the Crosby Arboretum Foundation in 1979.

The 58-acre site displays over 300 species of trees, shrubs, wildflowers and grasses indigenous to south-central Mississippi and Louisiana. Natural ecosystems represented include pitcher plant bog, natural slash-pine savanna, bottomland hardwood forest and cypress swamp.

Missouri

Shaw Arboretum
(of the Missouri Botanical Garden)

P.O. Box 38 (314) 577-5138
Gray Summit, MO 63039

Shaw Arboretum of the Missouri Botanical Garden, Gray Summit, Missouri

Hours: grounds, every day 7 to ½ hr. past sunset; Visitor Center, spring and fall, weekdays 8–4, weekends 9–4.
Admission: fee charged.
Directions: about 35 mi. southwest of St. Louis and south of Gray Summit; entrance is near the intersection of I–44 and State Hwy. 100.
Public Transportation: accessible by Trailways, Greyhound and Mid-American buses (Diamond stop).

Nearly four sq. mi., or 2,400 acres, of natural Ozark landscape form the Shaw Arboretum. Bordered on one side by the Meramec River, 1,800 acres are open to the public. Managed plantings include the 50-acre Pinetum and 60-acre prairie. A 12-mi. trail system allows visitors to enjoy the wooded sections of the Arboretum.

Jewel Box

Forest Park	(314) 534-9433
5600 Clayton	
St. Louis, MO 63110	

Hours: every day 9–5.

Admission: fee charged, except Mon. and Tues. 9–noon.
Directions: west on Hwy. 40 to Forest Park Zoo exit; enter Park on Hampton Ave. and Hwy. 40; Hampton to Wells Dr.; left on Wells, then left on McKinley Dr.

This unique structure, located in the city's largest park, was erected in 1936, and its design reflects the architectural style of that period. Six seasonal floral displays are staged each year in the 144 ft.–long, 55 ft.–wide and 50 ft.–tall Main Display Room. Tropical trees, foliage plants, waterfalls and fountains may be seen year-round.

Missouri Botanical Garden

Location:	(314) 577-5100
4344 Shaw Blvd.	**Mailing Address:**
St. Louis, MO 63110	P.O. Box 299
	St. Louis, MO 63166

Hours: every day 9–5; Memorial Day to Labor Day 9–8; closed Dec. 25.
Admission: fee charged.
Directions: south of I–44; take Kings Hwy. to Tower Grove Ave.; east on Tower Grove.
Public Transportation: accessible by bus.

The Missouri Botanical Garden, 79 acres of pools, fountains, specialty gardens and greenhouses, is the "oldest botanical garden in the U.S...established in 1859." It features over 5,000 kinds of plants and is listed as a National Historic Landmark.

The Climatron, a geodesic-dome conservatory covering one-half acre, is divided into four separate climatic environments. Orchids, bromeliads, carnivorous plants, tropical trees and other exotics are all displayed around a central waterfall. Other greenhouses include the Desert and Mediterranean Houses and Linnaean Greenhouse, which dates from 1881. The four glass structures cover 30,950 sq. ft.

Areas of interest outdoors include the Japanese Garden — surrounding a lake and featuring a teahouse, boulders, bridges and Japanese ornaments — two rose gardens, the Scented Garden, designed especially for the visually handicapped, and the English Woodland Garden. Tower Grove House, the former residence of Henry Shaw, founder of the Garden, is another attraction.

Shaw, an Englishman who made his fortune when St. Louis was still a pioneer town, started the Botanical Garden on the advice of prominent botanists Dr. Engelmann, Asa Gray and Sir Joseph Hooker, later director of the Royal Botanic Gardens at Kew. Shaw devoted the last 30 years of his life to this project. He died in 1899, leaving the Garden to be operated as a not-for-profit organization.

Nebraska

Nebraska Statewide Arboretum

111 Forestry Science Laboratory University of Nebraska Lincoln, NE 68508	(402) 472-2971

The Nebraska Statewide Arboretum is a unique concept uniting over 30 separate arboreta throughout Nebraska into a single administrative unit. The following, listed alphabetically, are all under the aegis of the statewide organization:

Alliance: Sallows Arboretum and Conservatory
Bellevue: Bellevue College Arboretum
Blair: Blair City Parks
    Dana College
Cedar Rapids: Cedar Rapids Public Schools Arboretum
Chadron: Chadron State College
Columbus: Elks Country Club Arboretum
Crete: Crete Public Schools Arboretum
    Doane College
Curtis: School of Technical Agriculture—Curtis Arboretum
Fremont: Luther Hormel Memorial Park
Halsey: Bessey Arboretum
Kearney: Cottonmill Park
    Kearney State College
Lincoln: Alice Abel Arboretum
    Chet Ager Nature Center
Earl Maxwell Arboretum, UNL East Campus
Hans Burchardt Arboretum
Joshua Turner Arboretum, Union College
Lincoln Regional Center Arboretum
Nebraska State Capitol Arboretum
Nebraska State Fairgrounds
Prairie Pines
Nebraska City: Arbor Lodge State Park (see descriptive entry)
North Platte: Glenn Viehmeyer Arboretum
Omaha: Elmwood Arboretum
Ord: Aagard Farm
Plattsmouth: Horning Farm
Scottsbluff: Panhandle Station Arboretum
Stanton: Maskenthine Lake and Recreation Area
Stromsburg: Midwest Park Arboretum
Wayne: Wayne State College

Arbor Lodge State Historical Park and Arboretum

Nebraska Game and Parks Commission Nebraska City, NE 68410	(402) 873-3221

Hours: grounds, every day 8–dusk; mansion, Apr. 15 to May 29, every day 1–5; May 30 to Sept. 7, every day 9–5; Sept. 8 to Oct., every day 1–5.
Admission: grounds, no fee; mansion, fee charged.

Directions: located at the west edge of Nebraska City, about one mi. from State Hwy. 73-75 and 2; Arbor Lodge turn is marked on both State Hwys.

In 1923 Joy Morton donated his 52-room, neo-colonial mansion, Arbor Lodge, and surrounding gardens and grounds to the State of Nebraska to be preserved as a monument to his father, J. Sterling Morton. The elder Morton settled in Nebraska City in 1855. Despite Nebraska's treeless plains, by 1858 the Mortons had established orchards and ornamental trees and shrubs on the grounds of their estate.

Joy Morton, the founder of Morton Salt, inherited Arbor Lodge from his father in 1902. He enlarged the mansion and built the elaborate Carriage House and Italian Terrace Garden. Originally planted by the Morton family, the Arboretum covers 65 acres and features over 250 species of trees and shrubs (thirteen trees are state champions). The Prairie Plants Garden, a display of native ornamental grasses and wildflowers, was established in recent years.

New Hampshire

Saint-Gaudens National Historic Site

RR #2, P.O. Box 73   (603) 675-2175
Cornish, NH 03745

Hours: last weekend in May to Oct., every day; grounds, 8–dusk; buildings, 8:30–4:30.
Admission: fee charged.
Directions: I-89, exit 20; I-91, exit 8.

The former home and studios of the American sculptor Augustus Saint-Gaudens (1848-1907) is landscaped with terrace gardens, hedge-lined garden enclosures, expanses of lawn and stands of trees. Statues and fountains accent the gardens, and trails wind through naturalized woodlands and wetlands. The property was deeded to a board of trustees in 1907, and in 1964 it was accepted as a gift by the National Park Service.

Fuller Gardens

10 Willow Ave.   (603) 964-5414
North Hampton, NH 03862

Hours: early May through Oct., every day 10–6.
Admission: fee charged.
Directions: I–95 to Rt. 1 exit; Rt. 1 to Rt. 101–D; follow 101–D east to junction with Rt. 1–A; go 200 yds. north on 1–A to Willow Ave.

Fuller Gardens, the summer home of the late Massachusetts Governor Alvan T. Fuller, preserves the horticultural beauty of an early 20th-century estate. Although the house no longer stands, the two-acre Gardens remain. These feature extensive plantings of roses set off by statuary and fountains, as well as a breathtaking ocean view. Additional highlights include the Japanese garden, wildflower walk, colorful perennial borders and annual beds enclosed by sculptured hedges and a conservatory filled with exotic tropical and desert plants.

The Gardens are maintained by the Fuller Foundation of New Hampshire.

Moffatt-Ladd House and Garden

154 Market St.   (603) 436-8221
Portsmouth, NH 03801

Hours: June 15 to Oct. 15, Mon.–Sat. 10–4, Sun. 2–5.
Admission: fee charged.
Directions: I–95 to Portsmouth; exit 7 (Market St.).

Although the Moffatt-Ladd House was built in 1763, the present garden design reflects the era of A.H. Ladd, who acquired the property in 1862. The House and grounds, designated as a National Historic Landmark in 1970, are maintained by the National Society of the Colonial Dames of America. The 2½-acre garden features brick walks, rose arbors, an herb garden, raised flower beds, grass steps, a grape arbor and old beehives. Old-fashioned perennials add to the historic atmosphere.

New Jersey

Leonard J. Buck Garden

Somerset County Park   **(201) 234-2677**
Commission
R.D. 2, Layton Rd.
Far Hills, NJ 07931

Hours: Mon.–Sat. 10–4; Sun. noon–4 (winter) and noon–6 (summer)
Admission: no fee.
Directions: from I–287, take the Bedminster exit onto Rt. 202; through Bedminster and Far Hills; turn right at Liberty Corner Rd.; continue 1 mi., turn right at Layton Rd.

The Leonard J. Buck Garden is a series of alpine and woodland gardens situated in a 33-acre stream valley. It was originally developed in the late 1930s by Leonard Buck as part of his estate. The plantings include an extensive collection of azaleas and rhododendrons, wildflowers, a fern collection, exotic alpines and rockery plants.

The Garden was donated by Mr. Buck's widow, Helen Buck, to the Somerset County Park Commission in 1976.

The Frelinghuysen Arboretum

53 East Hanover Ave.   **(201) 829-0474**
P.O. Box 1295R
Morristown, NJ 07960

Hours: weekdays, 9–4:30; weekends, March to May 30, 9–5, June to Labor Day, 10–6, Labor Day to Thanksgiving Day, 9–5.
Admission: no fee.
Directions: north on I–287 to exit 32A; Morris Ave. east to Whippany Rd.; left onto East Hanover Ave.; entrance on left opposite Morris County Library. South on I–287 to exit 32 to Ridgedale Ave.; right onto

Ridgedale, then right onto East Hanover Ave.; entrance on right.

The Frelinghuysen Arboretum consists of 127 acres divided into two tracts. The North Tract, made up of rich alluvial soil along the banks of the Whippany River, is under development as a demonstration area for public education. The South Tract is a varied, undulating terrain of swamp, forest and fields. Before becoming an Arboretum in 1971, the property was owned by the George Griswold Frelinghuysen family. Their former summer house, built in 1891, now serves as the Park Headquarters Administration Building for the Morris County Park Commission.

The demonstration area includes collections of lilacs, rhododendrons, azaleas, cherries, maples, hollies, conifers and viburnums. Other areas of interest are the Glossary Garden, Annual All-America Flower Garden, Rose Garden and Braille Nature Trail.

*Reeves-Reed Arboretum, Summit, New Jersey
(photo: Anne Ross)*

Willowwood Arboretum

P.O. Box 129R   **(201) 829-0474**
Morristown, NJ 07960

Hours: every day 9–4:30; closed Dec. through Feb.
Admission: no fee.
Directions: I–287 north to exit 18B; Rt. 206 north for 4 mi. to Pottersville Rd. (Rt. 512);

left on Pottersville, right on Union Grove Rd., left on Longview Rd.; entrance is on the left.

Willowwood Arboretum, on 130 acres of rolling farmland, contains about 3,500 kinds of native and exotic plants. Many of these date from the original plantings of brothers Henry and Robert Tubbs who bought the property in 1908. Two small formal gardens flank a residential structure that dates from 1792. But the pervading feeling of the site, which has been carefully developed over the years, is one of informal paths through open areas and woodland. Collections emphasized include oaks, maples, willows, lilacs, magnolias, hollies, cherries and conifers.

Willowwood was established as a private Arboretum in 1950 and became a unit of the Morris County Park System in 1980.

Rutgers University
Research and Display Gardens

P.O. Box 231   (201) 932-9325
Cook College
New Brunswick, NJ 08903

Hours: every day 7–dusk; closed Dec. 10 to Jan. 2.
Admission: no fee.
Directions: at junction of Ryder La. and U.S. Rt. 1; 1 mi. north of junction of Rt. 1 and 130 and 1 mi. south of junction of Rt. 1 and 18.

About 1,200 kinds of plants can be seen on the 30 acres of the Research and Display Gardens of Rutgers University open to the public. Special collections include hollies, yews, rhododendrons and other ericaceous plants. Demonstration hedges and vines and an Annual Garden present ideas for homeowners.

Now state supported, the Gardens were established in 1935 by Dr. Charles Connors.

Skylands

Ringwood State Park   (201) 962-7031
P.O. Box 302
Ringwood, NJ 07456

Hours: every day dawn–dusk.
Admission: fee charged.
Directions: New York State Thruway (I–87) to Rt. 17 north (at the I–87/287 interchange) to Sterling Mine Rd.; left at Shepard Lake Rd.
Public Transportation: Warwick Bus Line.

Skylands, dating from 1880, was once a private estate, with its gardens developed from 1920 to 1954 by Clarence McKenzie Lewis. Today, it is the only botanic garden in the New Jersey park system. Extending south from the manor house are Magnolia Walk and Octagonal, Azalea, Summer, Peony and Lilac Gardens. Other areas include the Pinetum, greenhouse and nursery, Dry Meadow, Swan Pond Meadow and Annual, Perennial, Bog, Rhododendron Display, Heather and Wildflower Gardens.

Duke Gardens Foundation, Inc.

P.O. Box 2030   (201) 722-3700
Hwy. 206 South
Somerville, NJ 08876

Hours: Oct. 1 to June 1, every day 12–4; advance reservation required; closed major holidays.
Admission: fee charged; school groups free Mon. and Fri.
Directions: located on Rt. 206, 17 mi. north of Princeton, 1½ mi. south of Somerville.

Duke Gardens is a unique collection of eleven greenhouses, each a full-scale re-creation of a garden of a particular style, country or period. These include: Chinese, Japanese, English, French, Italian, Indo-Persian, Colonial, Edwardian, American Desert and Tropical Jungle.

The Gardens were founded in 1960 when Doris Duke donated eleven acres of her estate, with existing greenhouses, to the Foundation. They opened as a public attraction in 1964.

The Reeves-Reed Arboretum

165 Hobart Ave.   (201) 273-8787
Summit, NJ 07901

Hours: every day 10–sunset.
Admission: no fee.
Directions: from Rt. 24 west take Hobart Ave. exit, turn left; entrance is second left off Hobart Ave. From Rt. 24 east, take Rt. 124 (service road) to Hobart Ave., turn right; entrance is second driveway on left.
Public Transportation: accessible by railroad and bus.

New York

Clark Garden

193 I. U. Willets Rd.   (516) 621-7568
Albertson, NY 11507

Hours: weekdays 8–4:30; Sat., Sun. and holidays 10–4:30; Garden Shop, Tues.– Thurs. and weekends 11–3.
Admission: fee charged.
Directions: L.I. Expressway to exit 37 south; Willis Ave. south one mi. to I.U. Willets Rd.; left on Willets; half a mi. to Garden entrance on left.
Public Transportation: accessible by bus and Long Island Railroad.

Clark Garden, a suburban branch of Brooklyn Botanic Garden, displays on its 12 wooded acres trees, shrubs and garden plants that are commercially available and best suited to local climate conditions. Emphasis is on uncommon plants, small flowering trees and early- and late-flowering shrubs.

The New York Botanical Garden

Bronx, NY 10458   (212) 220-8700

Hours: grounds, every day dawn–dusk; Conservatory, every day 10–4; closed Dec. 25, Jan. 1 and Thanksgiving Day.
Admission: fee charged for Conservatory and parking.
Directions: located in north–central Bronx; Bronx River Pkwy. passes the eastern boundary of the Garden; vehicle entrance is on Southern (Kazimiroff) Blvd., across from the entrance to Fordham University and near the Bronx Zoo.
Public Transportation: accessible by subway, bus and New York City Metro North Railroad.

The New York Botanical Garden (NYBG), a 250-acre oasis amid the urban hubbub of the Bronx, is an institution dedicated to plant-

Pond in the Arboretum at Cornell Plantations, Ithaca, New York (photo: Jon Crispin)

science research. The star of the horticultural attractions is the Enid A. Haupt Conservatory. Originally completed in 1901, the structure was entirely restored during 1976–78. The eleven houses form a rectangular complex covering 44,000 sq. ft. and hosting seasonal displays and a variety of plant collections. The latter comprise Tropical, Subtropical, Old World Desert, American Desert and Fern Forest, complete with waterfall and pool. The Palm Grove, the central domed house, is 90 ft. high and 100 ft. in diameter.

Highlights of the extensive grounds include: a Rose Garden (200 varieties); Rock Garden, with a re-created alpine scene; Pinetum; Herb Garden; and Native Plant Garden, with New Jersey pine-barrens area and spring-fed marsh. The NYBG Forest is a 40-acre preserve representing the only uncut woodland in New York City. The Museum Building houses the herbarium and 100,000-volume library.

Helping found the Garden in 1891, Nathaniel Lord Britton envisioned it as the American equivalent of the Royal Botanic Gardens at Kew. The Garden was given land in 1895, and ground was broken for the Conservatory in 1899.

New York Zoological Society—Bronx Zoo

Bronx River Pkwy.	(212) 367-1010
at Fordham Rd.	220-5141
Bronx, NY 10460	(tour reservations)

Hours: summer, Mon.–Sat. 10–5, Sun. and holidays 10–5:30; winter, every day 10–4:30.
Admission: fee charged; no fee Tues.–Thurs.
Directions: Bronx River Pkwy. to Bronx Zoo exit; follow signs.

Just opposite the New York Botanical Garden lies the Bronx Zoo—the largest urban installation of its kind in America—with 265 acres of woods, ponds, streams and parkland where 4,000 animals are in residence. Exhibits feature natural-habitat settings that include indigenous plantings.

The 38-acre "wilderness" of Wild Asia offers tigers, rhinoceros, antelope, exotic deer and elephants. The World of Birds building contains a tropical rain forest. Lions and antelope inhabit African Plains, and in Wild Asia's Jungle World, gibbons, monkeys and water monitors live in a setting that is the "most

Enid A. Haupt Conservatory, The New York Botanical Garden, Bronx, New York (photo: Alexandra Timchula)

ambitious indoor animal display ever attempted."

The New York Zoological Society opened the zoo in 1899.

Wave Hill

675 W. 252nd St.   (212) 549-2055
Bronx, NY 10471

Hours: every day 10–4:30.
Admission: no fee weekdays; fee charged weekends.
Directions: northbound on Henry Hudson Pkwy., exit at 246th St.; at 252nd St., turn left over the Pkwy. and left again; right at 249th St., straight to Wave Hill gate. South-bound on Henry Hudson Pkwy., exit at 254th St.; left at stop sign, left again at light; south to 249th St.; turn right, then straight ahead to gate.
Public Transportation: accessible by subway and bus.

Wave Hill, a Hudson River estate preserved for the public, sits on 28 acres, with the Hudson and the New Jersey Palisades forming a scenic backdrop. A turn-of-the-century atmosphere envelopes the houses and gardens of the property.

In 1893, when George Perkins, a wealthy financier, acquired the estate—including Wave Hill House, built in 1843—the gardens were laid out and surrounding properties (the nearby manor house Glyndor among them) were added.

Today, Wave Hill House shelters a series of changing exhibits. The 2,000 sq. ft. Conservatory encompasses seasonal floral displays and collections of cacti and succulents and tropicals. Other points of interest, both indoors and out, include the Flower Garden, Herb Garden, English-style Wild Garden, Aquatic Garden, Thematic Plant Exhibit and Alpine House. Below the formal-garden area, is a ten-acre stretch of woodland.

The site remained in private use until 1960 when it was given to the City. For the management of the property, Wave Hill, Inc. was formed in 1965.

Brooklyn Botanic Garden

1000 Washington Ave.   (718) 622-4433
Brooklyn, NY 11225

Hours: grounds, May–Sept. weekdays 8–6, weekends and holidays 10–6; Oct.–Apr., weekdays 8–4:30, weekends and holidays 10–4:30; Japanese Garden hours change according to the season; Garden Shop, Apr.–Sept., weekdays 9:30–5:30, weekends and holidays 10–5:30; Oct.–Mar., weekdays 9:30–4:30, weekends and holidays 10–4:30; closed Thanksgiving Day, Dec. 25 and Jan. 1; grounds and Shop closed Mon.
Admission: grounds, no fee (donations accepted); Japanese Garden, fee charged weekends and holidays.
Directions: in Brooklyn, next to Prospect Park and Brooklyn Museum; from the north, Triborough Bridge to Brooklyn-Queens Expwy. (278); exit at Atlantic Ave., right at Washington Ave.; from the south, Staten Island Expwy. (278), across Verrazano Narrows Bridge, to Prospect Expwy.; exit at Fort Hamilton Pkwy., left at Caton Ave., left at Ocean Ave., left at Washington Ave.
Public Transportation: accessible by subway.

Between Prospect Park and the Brooklyn Museum, 52 acres, displaying over 12,000 kinds of plants, comprise Brooklyn Botanic Garden (BBG). Escape from bustling city streets is offered by a variety of specialized gardens. The Japanese Hill-and-Pond Garden is particularly tranquil. Built in 1914, it contains several Japanese-style structures and ornaments. The formal Cranford Rose Garden's more than 5,000 plants of 900 cultivars may be viewed in its entirety from atop the Overlook. From the same high vantage point, Cherry Esplanade may be admired. In full bloom each spring, this allée of Japanese cherry trees draws crowds of visitors to the Garden.

The Japanese Hill-and-Pond Garden, Brooklyn Botanic Garden, Brooklyn, New York (photo: George Malave)

Other areas of interest include: the Rock Garden; Fragrance Garden for the Blind; Magnolia Plaza; Shakespeare Garden; Herb Garden; Rhododendron Garden; Osborne Memorial Section; Local Flora Section, containing only those plants native to the area within a 100-mile radius of New York City; and the Children's Garden, representing the vegetable- and flower-growing efforts of over 300 young people each summer.

BBG was established in 1910 by a group of citizens interested in developing a public garden. Land for the project was leased by the City. Today, the Garden is overseen by Brooklyn Botanic Garden, Inc., a private organization. The Administration Building, designed in Italian-Renaissance style by McKim, Mead & White, has been designated a Historic Landmark. A new $21-million conservatory complex is scheduled to open in 1988.

Sonnenberg Gardens

P.O. Box 663   (716) 394-4922
Canandaigua, NY 14424

Hours: May 10 to mid–Oct., every day 9:30–5:30.
Admission: fee charged.
Directions: near New York State Thruway exits 43 and 44; located at 151 Charlotte off Rt. 21 north (E. Gibson St.); 1 mi. east of Main St. in Canandaigua.

George Landis Arboretum

Esperance, NY 12066   (518) 875-6935

Hours: Apr.–Nov., every day sunrise–sunset.
Admission: no fee.
Directions: located 30 mi. west of Albany, on Rt. 20, two mi. north of Esperance.

Over 2,000 kinds of herbaceous and woody plants may be seen at the George Landis Arboretum. The 96-acre site features a rose garden, rock garden, wildflower area, conifers, lilacs, rhododendrons and flowering crabapples. The Arboretum was founded in 1951 by Fred Lape.

Queens Botanical Garden

43-50 Main St.   **(718) 886-3800**
Flushing, NY 11355

Hours: every day 8–sundown.
Admission: no fee (contributions accepted).
Directions: College Point exit off Van Wyck Expwy.; Main St. exit off Long Island Expwy. (past Booth Memorial Hospital).
Public Transportation: accessible by IRT subway (#7); Main St. stop.

The Queens Botanical Garden, situated on 39 acres in a densely populated metropolitan area, strives to serve homeowners and plant lovers in the surrounding community. Formal landscaped areas include: the rose collection, featuring over 5,000 plants; six backyard demonstration gardens, offering ideas for a small urban plot; the Rock Garden; and the Herb Garden. Collections of crabapples, cherries, maples, magnolias and historic trees and shrubs of Flushing dot the parklike arboretum section of the Garden.

The Queens Botanical Garden Society was established in 1946. In 1960 the Garden was moved from its original location to make room for the 1964–65 World's Fair. It opened at its present site in 1963.

Cornell Plantations

1 Plantations Rd.   **(607) 256-3020**
Ithaca, NY 14850

Hours: grounds, every day sunrise–sunset; headquarters building, weekdays 8–4, weekends 12–4.
Admission: no fee.
Directions: off Rt. 366 in Ithaca.
Public Transportation: accessible by bus.

Cornell Plantations, combining features of an arboretum, botanical garden and natural preserve, is made up of 2,800 acres of steep gorges, ponds, streams, woodland, hilly terrain, swamp areas and specialized gardens. Eleven off-campus natural areas contribute to the Plantations' total acreage.

Specialized areas include: Robison York State Herb Garden; Heasley Rock Garden; American Peony Society Garden; International Crops and Weed Garden; Rhododendron, Ground cover, Rose and Heritage Crops Collections; and Lath House.

The Plantations began in 1935 when University administrators and professors saw the need for an outdoor laboratory for students and the general public.

Bailey Arboretum

Bayville Rd.   **(516) 676-4497**
Locust Valley, NY 11560

Hours: mid–April to mid–Nov., every day 9–4; closed Mon.
Admission: fee charged.
Directions: from intersection of Rt. 25A and Wolver Hollow Rd. (Brookville Police Station), follow signs for Arboretum.

Formerly the summer home of Mr. and Mrs. Frank Bailey, the 42 acres and house (built in the 1800s) that make up Bailey Arboretum were given to Nassau County in 1968 and are maintained by the Department of Recreation and Parks. Outstanding features are an iris garden, rose garden, perennial border, rock garden and a collection of over 600 kinds of trees and shrubs, including many rare species.

The John P. Humes Japanese Stroll Garden

347 Oyster Bay Rd.   **(516) 676-4486**
Locust Valley, NY 11560

Admission: fee charged.
Directions: Long Island Expwy. exit 39N to Rt. 25A (Northern Blvd.); turn right and go 3 mi. to Wolver Hollow Rd., turn left to end, turn right on Chicken Valley Rd.; proceed 1.8 mi. to Dogwood La., turn right. Entrance is 200 ft. on right.

Public Transportation: Long Island Railroad to Locust Valley, then taxi (2 mi.).

Innisfree Garden

Tyrrel Rd.	**(914) 677-8000**
Millbrook, NY 12545	

Hours: May–Oct., weekends 11–5, Wed.–Fri. 10–4; closed Mon. and Tues.; open Mon. legal holidays.
Admission: weekends, fee charged; weekdays, no fee.
Directions: on Tyrrel Rd. 1 mi. from Rt. 44; 2½ mi. from South Millbrook on Rt. 44, turn left on Tyrrel Rd.; 1¾ mi. from Taconic Pkwy. overpass on Rt. 44, turn right on Tyrrel Rd.

Innisfree Garden comprises a 180-acre basin of "naturalized" gardens and woodland surrounding a picturesque lake. Walter Beck, the Garden's creator, was a student of Oriental art. Beginning in 1930 and using eastern design principles, he worked for 22 years staking out streams, walkways and plantings. The terraces, retaining walls, sculptural groupings of natural rock, waterfalls and planned vistas of the lake were organized to keep elements "in tension," or "in motion."

The Garden was given to the Innisfree Foundation in 1959.

Mary Flagler Cary Arboretum
Institute of Ecosystem Studies

Box AB	**(914) 677-5358**
Millbrook, NY 12545	

Hours: Mon.–Sat. 9–4, Sun. 1–4; closed holidays.
Admission: no fee; obtain a Visitor Access Permit at the Gifford House Visitor and Education Center.
Directions: located 75 mi. north of New York City; Taconic Pkwy. to Rt. 44 east; two mi. to 44A; after one mi., Gifford House is the second building on the left.

The Mary Flagler Cary Arboretum property was acquired in 1971 by The New York Botanical Garden. It is now the site of the Institute of Ecosystem Studies. Formerly the estate of Mrs. Mary Flagler Cary, the Arboretum was established in her memory by a trust.

Features include: five miles of paved road and two nature trails; the Gifford House (built in 1817), containing a small reference library and Gift and Plant Shop; the Perennial Garden, offering examples of low-maintenance choices; 60 cultivars of lilacs; the Greenhouse, where visitors may see tropical plants and propagation techniques; and the Fern Glen, displaying an extensive collection of hardy ferns from Europe, Japan, the Soviet Union, Mexico and parts of North America.

The Astor Court, The Metropolitan Museum of Art, New York. (The installation made possible through the generosity of the Vincent Astor Foundation.)

Leon McDonald

A Collection
of Gardens

Japanese Garden,
Goldsmith Civic Garden Center,
Memphis Tennessee

Fairchild
Tropical Garden,
Miami, Florida

Claire Sawyers

Claire Sawyers

Magnolia Plaza and
Administration Building,
Brooklyn Botanic Garden,
Brooklyn, New York

Elvin McDonald

Missouri Botanical Garden,
St. Louis, Missouri

Dixon Gallery and Gardens,
Memphis, Tennessee

Elvin McDonald

Old Westbury Gardens, Westbury, Long Island, New York

San Francisco Park Conservatory, San Francisco, California

Elvin McDonald

**Blithewold Gardens and Arboretum,
Bristol, Rhode Island**

**Longwood Gardens Conservatory,
Kennett Square, Pennsylvania**

Claire Sawyers

Sonnenberg Gardens, Canadaigua, New York

Mohonk Mountain House

New Paltz, NY 12561　　　**(914) 255-1000**

Admission: fee charged; no fee for House guests.
Directions: six mi. west of New Paltz; New York State Thruway to exit 18; left at Rt. 299; after crossing the Wallkill River, turn right, bear left at the next "Y" and follow Mountain Rest Rd.
Public Transportation: shuttle bus from bus station in New Paltz.

Mohonk Mountain House is a Victorian-inspired resort made up of 25,000 acres of unspoiled countryside and a crystal-clear lake. Surrounding the House, 15 acres of gardens feature extensive annual and perennial borders, a rock garden, wildflower-fern trail, rose garden, herb garden, greenhouses and specimen trees and shrubs. A five-day Garden Holiday program, with lectures and demonstrations, is scheduled each year. The House opened to guests in 1870 and, today, can accommodate as many as 500.

The Astor Court

Department of　　　　　**(212) 879-5500**
Far Eastern Art
Metropolitan Museum of Art
5th Ave. at 82nd St.
New York, NY 10028

Hours: Wed.–Sun. 9:30–5:15; Tues. 9:30–8:45; closed Mon.
Admission: contribution suggested.
Directions: 5th Ave. at 82nd St.; parking available in Museum garage at 80th St.
Public Transportation: accessible by Lexington Ave. subway; use 86th (express) or 78th St. (local) stops; bus routes 1, 2, 3, 4, 17 or 18.

The Biblical Garden at the Cathedral of St. John the Divine

1047 Amsterdam Ave.　　　**(212) 678-6886**
New York, NY 10025　　　　　**864-3760**

Hours: every day 9–sunset.
Admission: no fee.
Directions: Westside Hwy. to 96th St. exit, north to 110th St.; east on 110th St. to Amsterdam Ave., north again to 112th St.
Public Transportation: accessible by New York City bus and subway.

The Biblical Garden at the Cathedral of St. John the Divine, New York City

The Cloisters

The Metropolitan   **(212) 923-3700**
Museum of Art
Fort Tryon Park
New York, NY 10040

Hours: Mar.–Oct., Tues.–Sun. 9:30–5:15; Nov.–Feb., Tues.–Sun. 9:30–4:45; closed Mon., Thanksgiving Day, Dec. 25 and Jan 1.

Admission: donation requested.
Directions: from Manhattan, Henry Hudson Pkwy. north to the first exit after the George Washington Bridge.
Public Transportation: accessible by Madison Ave. bus #4; also, 8th Ave. subway "A" train to 190th St., then bus #4 to the Cloisters.

The Cloisters, a branch of The Metropolitan Museum of Art, presents examples of medieval art, architecture and cloister gardens. On a bluff overlooking the Hudson River, a single structure incorporates sections of a 12th-century chapter house, the cloisters of five medieval monasteries and a Romanesque chapel. The gardens are planted with materials grown in western Europe during the Middle Ages (800–1520 A.D.).

On the ground floor are the Bonnefont and Trie Cloisters. The former's two arcades of white marble capitals enclose a medieval herb garden. The Trie Cloister garden features plants that are depicted in the famous *Hunt of the Unicorn* tapestries, in the collection of the Museum. An indoor spring garden surrounds a fountain in the Saint-Guilhem Cloister. Fragrant plants are grown in the courtyard garden of the Cuxa Cloister.

The building and the art collection it houses were funded by John D. Rockefeller, Jr. The Cloisters opened to the public in 1938.

The Conservatory Garden, Central Park

830 Fifth Ave.	(212) 360-8236
New York, NY 10021	

Hours: 8–dusk.
Admission: no fee.
Directions: located at 105th St. and Fifth Ave., on the edge of Central Park.
Public Transportation: accessible by Fifth Ave. bus; Lexington Ave. subway to 103rd St.

The Conservatory Garden features six acres of formal plantings, with hundreds of roses, a wisteria pergola, crabapple allées, bulbs, perennial borders and three water installa-

tions. Built on the former site of a series of conservatories, the Garden opened 1937 and was recently restored by the Central Park Conservancy.

Bayard Cutting Arboretum

P.O. Box 466	(516) 581-1002
Montauk Hwy.	
Oakdale, NY 11709	

Hours: Wed.–Sun. 10–5; open legal holidays.
Admission: fee charged, except during winter months.
Directions: Southern State Pkwy. (Heckscher Pkwy.), exit 45 east to Montauk Hwy.; entrance is on Montauk Hwy., one mi. east of Pkwy.
Public Transportation: accessible by Long Island Railroad to Islip Station, then taxi (3 mi.) to the Arboretum; MSBA bus rt. S40 serves Montauk Hwy.

Bayard Cutting Arboretum sits on a 690-acre strip of land along the Connetquot River. It was developed in the late 1800s as the private residence of Mr. and Mrs. Bayard Cutting. In 1952 Mrs. Cutting gave the estate to the Long Island State Park and Recreation Commission. About 1,200 kinds of plants may be seen on the 130 acres open to the public.

The Arboretum's naturalistic design was laid out by Frederick Law Olmsted in 1887 and is listed in the Register of Historic Landmarks. Although the site suffered severe hurricane damage in 1985, many specimens that date back to the original plantings survive in the Pinetum. These include fir, spruce, pine, cypress, cedar, yew and hemlock trees. Among the numerous pathways available, five recommended routes are outlined for visitors: Pinetum Walk, Wildflower Walk, Rhododendron Walk, Bird Watcher's Walk and Swamp Cypress Walk.

Old Westbury Gardens

P.O. Box 430
Old Westbury, NY 11568

Hours: May–Oct., Wed.–Sun. and all holidays 10–5; April and Nov., Sun. 11–4.
Admission: separate fees for house and Gardens.

Directions: Long Island Expwy. to exit 39S; 1¼ mi. east on service rd.; ¼ mi. south on Old Westbury Rd.

Public Transportation: Long Island Railroad to Westbury Station; taxi (2 mi.) from there.

Old Westbury Gardens maintains the same 18th-century English country estate atmosphere it evoked as the private residence of the late John S. Phipps. Built in 1906, the Charles II-style manor house and display garden are the creation of George Crawley, a London designer and collector. Listed in the National Register of Historic Places, the 70-acre estate is preserved as an example of the grandeur of the early 20th century.

Distinct garden areas lie on both sides of the formal, hedge-lined axis behind the mansion. Boxwood, already 100 years old when it was planted 50 years ago, borders the reflecting pool in the Boxwood Garden. Lilac Walk leads to the Walled Garden, famous for its extensive herbaceous borders; 1½ acres of floral displays complement ornamental pools, fountains and arbors in this enclosed area. The Pinetum and sunken Rose Garden are nearby. In addition, contemporary demonstration gardens provide visitors with practical ideas for their own gardens. Woodland Walk loops around the lake to the Temple of Love and back to the manor house. Inside the stately residence, rooms filled with art objects and English antiques remain as they were over 75 years ago.

In 1959 the Phipps family established a foundation to preserve the estate.

Planting Fields Arboretum

Planting Fields Rd.   (516) 922-9201
Oyster Bay, NY 11771

Hours: grounds, every day 10–5; greenhouses, every day 10–4:30; closed Dec. 25.
Admission: fee charged weekends and holidays year-round and every day May 1 to Labor Day.
Directions: Long Island Expwy. to exit 41 north; Rt. 106 (Jericho-Oyster Bay Rd.) to Rt. 25A; left (west) on 25A; right on Mill River Rd.; north to Glen Cove Rd.; left on Planting Fields Rd.; entrance is on the left.

Once the private estate of William Coe, Planting Fields Arboretum is 400 acres of formal and informal gardens containing about 6,500 kinds of plants.

Coe Hall, the manor house on the property, is a fine example of Elizabethan architecture. To the north, 40 acres of lawn and large specimen trees immediately set off the mansion. To the south are the camellia greenhouse (over 100 varieties) and the main greenhouse complex, featuring six changing floral displays each year. Rhododendron Park encompasses an extensive collection of more than 800 species and hybrids. The five-acre Synoptic Garden, an alphabetically arranged collection of shrubs, contains over 400 superior species and cultivars. The Dwarf Conifer Garden, Formal Gardens, Wildflower Garden and Bird Sanctuary are other areas of interest.

William Coe died in 1955, after bequeathing the horticultural showplace he had developed over his lifetime to the people of New York State. Today, the Arboretum is registered as a Historic District and is administered by the Long Island State Park Commission.

Highland Park

Monroe County Parks   (716) 244-4640
Arboretum
375 Westfall Rd.
Rochester, NY 14620

New York Zoological Society-Bronx Zoo,
Bronx, New York (photo: New York Zoological
Society photo)

Hours: every day dawn to dusk; conservatory, every day 9:30–5.
Admission: no fee.
Directions: 1 mi. south of Goodman St. exit off I–490; south of downtown Rochester; bordered by South Ave., Highland Ave. and Goodman St.
Public Transportation: accessible by bus.

Highland Park is most famous for its Festival of Lilacs, but the 155-acre park has about 2,500 different kinds of plants.

The park is an arboretum of mature plantings including rhododendrons, azaleas, viburnums, forsythias, magnolias, mock-oranges, and cherries. The Pinetum contins mature and unusual pines, firs, and other evergreens, some of which have passsed their 100th birthday. The lilacs, the highlight in May, are a display of over 1,200 shrubs of 500 varieties covering 22 acres. Tulip beds (15,000 bulbs) and a pansy bed (10,000 plants arranged in a design) add to the May festivities. (The festival starts the third Sunday in May, runs for 10 days).

Lamberton Conservatory (5,400 sq. feet), within the park, dates back to 1911. It houses seasonal exhibits, tropical foliage plants, orchids and cacti and succulents.

Highland Park started in 1888 when Ellwanger and Barry Nursery donated 20 acres to the community which soon became famed as one of the nation's first great municipal arboreta. The lilac collection was established in 1892 when John Dunbar gave 20 varieties.

North Carolina

Biltmore House and Gardens

Asheville, NC 28802   (704) 274-1776
For further info. contact:
The Biltmore Co. Marketing Dept.
1 Biltmore Plaza
Asheville, NC 28802

Hours: every day 9–5; closed Thanksgiving Day, Dec. 25 and Jan. 1.
Admission: fee charged for various tours.

Biltmore House and Gardens, Asheville, North Carolina

Directions: located on U.S. 23, 3 blocks north of exit 50 or 50B on I–40 in Asheville.

Biltmore House, the former home of George Vanderbilt (grandson of "Commodore" Vanderbilt) is modeled after the great chateaux of France. The formal gardens are based specifically on those of Vaux-le-Vicomte. The 250-acre parklike landscape surrounding the mansion is probably one of the best-preserved designs of Frederick Law Olmsted.

The outstanding horticultural features of this National Historic Landmark include: the Victorian Conservatory, a three-wing structure covering over 7,000 sq. ft.; the four-acre, English-style Walled Garden; the Azalea Garden, an extensive collection of native, deciduous varieties; the 3,000-plant Rose Garden; the Italian Garden, with three pools containing aquatic plants; and the Shrub Garden, where paths wind among flowering trees and shrubs. Potted plants decorate many of the mansion's 250 lavishly appointed rooms, but they reign supreme in Palm Court, a sunken conservatory within the house.

After George Vanderbilt's death in 1914, a large portion of the estate's 125,000 acres was deeded to the government to form Pisgah

National Forest. In 1930 Mr. Vanderbilt's only child Cornelia, together with her husband, opened the House and Gardens to the public. Today, the estate comprises 8,000 acres.

University Botanical Gardens at Asheville, Inc.

| University of North Carolina—Asheville W.T. Weaver Blvd. Asheville, NC 28804 | (704) 252-5190 (Visitor Center) |

Hours: every day dawn–dusk.
Admission: no fee.
Directions: I–240 to Expwy. (U.S. 19, 23, 70) north; exit at Broadway (south); left on W.T. Weaver Blvd.

Ten acres devoted to the preservation and display of flora native to North Carolina make up the University Botanical Gardens at Asheville. The land is owned by the University, but has been entrusted to the University Botanical Gardens Association for development.

Displaying 750 kinds of plants from all parts of North Carolina, the Gardens include the Sunshine Garden, Bog Garden, Azalea Garden, Founder's Award Rock Garden, Garden for the Blind, Heath Cove and Sycamore Area, with trails, three streams and natural rock outcroppings. The institution also acts as a testing ground for new plants considered for introduction into the area.

The University Botanical Gardens were founded in 1960 with the help of the Asheville Garden Club.

The North Carolina Botanical Garden

| UNC-CH Totten Center 457-A Chapel Hill, NC 27514 | (919) 967-2246 |

Hours: Mon.–Fri. 8–5, except winter holi-

days; mid–Mar. to mid–Nov., Sat. 10–5, Sun. 2–5.
Admission: no fee.
Directions: on Laurel Hill Rd., just south of U.S. 15–501 and 54 bypass in Chapel Hill.

The North Carolina Botanical Garden's main visitor area features collections of native southeastern plants (arranged according to habit) and more than two mi. of trails through Piedmont woodland. Highlights include displays of wildflowers, ferns, carnivorous and aquatic plants, plus an herb garden and plant-families garden. The NCBG is committed to the conservation of native plants through natural-area preservation and propagation.

Included in the 525-acre installation are the five-acre Coker Arboretum and 352-acre Mason Biological Farm. The Arboretum, on campus, has significant plantings of dwarf conifers, daffodils, Asian species, rhododendron and azalea cultivars and daylilies. It was originally designed in 1903, and today displays 1,000 kinds of plants.

The Van Landingham Glen and Susie Harwood Garden

| Biology Department University of North Carolina at Charlotte Charlotte, NC 28223 | (704) 597-4055 |

Hours: every day 8–dark.
Admission: no fee.
Directions: 9 mi. northeast of the center of Charlotte, on Rt. 49; on the UNCC campus.
Public Transportation: accessible by city bus from downtown Charlotte.

Sarah P. Duke Gardens

| Duke University Durham, NC 22706 | (919) 684-3698 |

Hours: every day 8–dark.
Admission: no fee.
Directions: adjacent to Duke University and Medical Center; main entrance is on Anderson St.

About 1,500 kinds of plants adorn the 15 acres of formal and informal gardens that comprise Duke University's Sarah P. Duke Gardens. The formal Terraced Garden, sloping down to a pond, is the focal centerpiece. Stone-terraced beds, stretching out on either side of a broad stairway, are softened with flowering and ever-green trees, mixed with showy bulbs and annuals through spring and summer. The contrasting Blomquist Garden, set in a natural woodland, is limited to native plants. The Rose Garden, Azalea Court, Wisteria Pergola, Rock Garden, Asian Plant Collection and Iris Garden are other features.

The Gardens originated in 1932, when Dr. Hanes of Duke University Hospital gained financial support for their development from Sarah Duke. The installation opened to the public in 1934.

Tryon Palace Restoration and Garden Complex

P.O. Box 1007   **(919) 638-5109**
610 Pollock St.
New Bern, NC 28560

Hours: Mon.–Sat. 9:30–5, Sun. 1:30–5; closed Thanksgiving Day, Dec. 24–26 and Jan. 1.
Admission: fee charged.
Directions: 90 mi. east of I–95 on U.S. 70; U. S. 17 also passes through New Bern; in Historic New Bern, at the intersection of Pollock and George Sts.

North Carolina State University Arboretum

Department of Horticultural   (919) 737-3132
Science

University Botanical Gardens at Asheville, Inc., North Carolina (photo: Dr. Robert T. Kemp)

North Carolina State University
Raleigh, NC 27695

Hours: every day dawn–dusk.
Admission: no fee.
Directions: near the State Fairgrounds; take Hillsborough St. exit off I–64 Bypass; west on Hillsborough; take first crossing (left) over railroad tracks, then left at Beryl Rd.; located on Beryl Rd.

The eight-acre NCSU Arboretum, displaying about 5,000 kinds of trees, shrubs, vines, flowering plants, ground covers and grasses, was begun in 1976. Highlights include a home-landscape idea garden and a 300 ft.–long perennial border.

The Horticultural Science Greenhouses and Conservatory (open Mon.–Fri. 8–12 and 1–5; 919-737-3131), on the NCSU campus behind Kilgor Hall, is the University's teaching and research greenhouse (30,000 sq. ft.). Here the public may see over 900 species, including peperomia, cryptanthus and miniature-ivy collections.

Orton Plantation Gardens

RFD 1   **(919) 371-6851**
Winnabow, NC 28479

Hours: Mar.–Aug., every day 8–6; Sept.–Nov., 8–5.
Admission: fee charged.
Directions: 18 mi. south of Wilmington on State Hwy. 133.

Orton Plantation Gardens encompass 20 acres surrounding Orton House, a southern antebellum mansion. Live oaks, magnolias, cypress and pine trees are emphasized, and spacious lawns and ponds provide settings for thousands of azaleas, camellias and annuals. The Gardens opened to the public in the mid-1930s.

Old Salem, Inc.

Drawer F, Salem Station   **(919) 723-3688**
Winston-Salem, NC 27108

Hours: Mon.–Sat. 8:30–4:30; closed Dec. 25.
Admission: fee charged.
Directions: located in downtown Winston-Salem, off I–40.
Public Transportation: accessible by bus.

Old Salem, a Moravian congregation-town restoration, covers 40 acres and features nine buildings dating from 1760 to 1840. The various structures are filled with period furnishings and household items, and are set in a re-created 18th-century landscape with gardens. Heirloom fruit trees, grapes, roses and shrubs, as well as old varieties of annuals, bulbs, perennials, vegetables and herbs—all authentic to the time—are grown in the Family Gardens. Altogether, about 1,000 kinds of plants embellish the restored landscape.

The historic value of the site was recognized in 1947, and as a means of preserving and restoring it, Old Salem, Inc., a not-for-profit organization, was established.

Reynolda Gardens of Wake Forest University

100 Reynolda Village   **(919) 761-5593**
Winston-Salem, NC 27106

Hours: grounds, every day sunrise-sunset; greenhouses and Conservatory, Mon.–Fri 9–3, open weekends for special shows; Reynolda House, Tues.–Sat. 9–4:30, Sun. 1–4:30.
Admission: Gardens, no fee; Reynolda House, fee charged.
Directions: adjacent to Wake Forest University campus; from I–40 take Silas Creek Pkwy. north; right (east) at Reynolda Rd.; enter Reynolda Village main entrance.

Reynolda Gardens, 129 acres of formal and "natural" plantings, were built in 1916 as part of the estate of R.J. Reynolds, founder of the Reynolds Tobacco Company. They were donated to Wake Forest University between 1958 and 1962 by the Mary Reynolds Babcock Foundation.

Four-and-a-half acres of formal gardens fronting the Conservatory feature plantings of boxwood, annual and perennial beds. The grounds' central axis leads through the Upper Gardens which contain vegetables, fruits, flowers for cutting and an All-America Rose Garden. The third area, the Greater Gardens, is 125 acres of open fields and natural woodland. A wide variety of native flora and wildlife may be viewed on the nature trail leading to Lake Katherine. The Lord and Burnham Conservatory (dating from 1912) displays a variety of tropical plants, and Reynolda House shelters a collection of American art.

North Dakota

International Peace Garden

Dunseith, ND 58329   **(701) 263-4390**
                           P.O. Box 419
                           Boissevain, Manitoba
                           Canada R0K 0E0

The International Peace Garden, dedicated in 1932, commemorates over 150 years of peaceful relations between the U.S. and Canada. The 2,400-acre site boasts scenic drives, nature trails through wooded lake country, an arboretum maintained by the

Manitoba Horticultural Association and formal gardens that include a floral clock. Additional highlights are fountain displays and plantings of roses and All-America annuals. Structures of interest include the Peace Tower, Carillon Bell Tower, Peace Chapel, Amphitheater, Lodge, Legion Athletic Camp and Masonic Auditorium. The Willis Centennial Pavilion, with exhibits and dining facilities, serves as a visitor center.

The Professional Grounds Management Society was the Peace Garden's founding organization.

Ohio

Stan Hywet Hall and Gardens

714 North Portage Path   (216) 836-5533
Akron, Oh 44303

Hours: Tues.–Sat. 10–4; Sun. 1–4; closed Mon. and major national holidays.
Admission: fee charged.
Directions: twenty minutes south of the Ohio Turnpike (exits 11 or 12), via I–77, Rt. 8, I–71 or I–271; these all intersect with Rt. 18 (Market St.); Portage Path runs north off Rt. 18.

Stan Hywet Hall, a 65-room manor house of Tudor Revival style, surrounded by 70 acres of gardens, meadows, woods and lagoons, was originally designed by landscape architect Warren Manning. The estate was built in 1915 by Frank A. Seiberling, founder of the Goodyear and Seiberling Rubber Companies. After his death in 1955, his heirs, along with Akron Civic leaders, formed a foundation to operate the Hall as a self-supporting museum and cultural center. It is listed in the National Register of Historic Places and is a National Historic Landmark.

The forty acres of the grounds under intensive cultivation include the Rose Garden, Peony Beds (300 varieties), Plum Tree Garden, Alpine Garden, Cutting Gardens, Daylily Beds and Grape Arbor. The tree-lined approach road borders the Great Meadow, a vast open space spotted with naturalized daffodils and 20,000 tulips in spring and 10,000 chrysanthemums in late summer. The restored green-houses and conservatory stand at the edge of the Gardens. Inside the Hall, rooms are appointed with Stuart and Tudor funishings.

Cemetery of Spring Grove

4521 Spring Grove Ave.   (513) 681-6680
Cincinnati, OH 45232

Hours: grounds, every day 8–5; office, Mon.–Fri. 8–4:30, Sat. 8–noon; Memorial Mausoleum, every day 10–4.
Admission: no fee.
Directions: Four mi. north of downtown Cincinnati; 1 mi. west of I–75; take Mitchell Ave. exit west to the first intersection; turn left onto Spring Grove Ave.; ½ mi. to main entrance.

Civic Garden Center of Greater Cincinnati and The Hauck Botanic Garden

2715 Reading Rd.   (513) 221-0981
Cincinnati, OH 45206

Hours: Garden Center, Tues.–Sat. 9–3; closed major holidays and Dec. 20 to Jan. 20; Hauck Botanic Garden, Mon.–Fri. 10–4.
Admission: no fee.
Directions: two blocks from I–71; William Howard Taft exit to Reading Rd.; one block north.
Public Transportation: accessible by bus.

Krohn Conservatory

Eden Park   (513) 352-4090
Eden Park Dr.   352-4091
Cincinnati, OH 45202   (tour reservations)

Hours: Mon.–Sat. 10–5, Sun. 10–6; Easter Sunday 7 a.m. to 10 p.m.; Easter week and Dec. 25 10 a.m. to 9 p.m.; Gift Shop, every day 10–5, closed holidays.

Admission: no fee.
Directions: from downtown, 2 mi. northeast of Gilbert Ave.; turn into Eden Park; about 1 mi. on Eden Park Dr. to Conservatory. East on U.S. 50, exit Martin St. to Eden Park Dr.; Conservatory is at the corner of Martin St. and Eden Park Dr.; from I–71 (north or south), exit at Elsinor Ave. or Florence Ave. and follow signs.

With nearly 24,000 sq. ft. under glass, the Krohn Conservatory, offering a tour of a tropical rain forest, is Cincinnati's horticultural showcase. In addition to permanent displays of palms, cacti, citrus trees, ferns and orchids in naturalistic settings, six seasonal floral shows are staged annually.

The Conservatory opened in 1933 as a facility of the Cincinnati Park Board.

Mt. Airy Arboretum

5083 Colerain Ave.   (513) 541-8176
Cincinnati, OH 45239

Hours: every day 7:30–sunset.
Admission: no fee.
Directions: I–75 to I–74 west; exit at Colerain Ave.; 1 mi. north on Colerain to entrance of Mt. Airy Forest; follow signs to Arboretum.
Public Transportation: accessible by bus.

Mt. Airy Arboretum is made up of 120 acres planted with more than 1,200 different species. Its collection of trees and shrubs includes ash, birch, beech, buckeye, cherry, crabapple, deutzia, dogwood, elm, euonymus, fir, hawthorn, hemlock, juniper, lilac, magnolia, maple, oak, poplar, spruce, viburnum, willow and yew. Outstanding displays are those of dwarf conifers, perennials and azaleas. A number of specialty gardens punctuate the landscape: the Meyer Lake and Rara Flora Garden, with rare and unusual plantings around the one-acre lake; the Garden of the Rhododendron and the Braam Memorial Garden, featuring azaleas and rhododendrons; and the Green Garden, emphasizing demonstration plantings of shrubs, ground covers, vines and herbs.

The Mt. Airy Arboretum was established in 1932 by the Cincinnati Park Board, with help from the National Federation of Garden Clubs. It is located within the 1,466 acres of Mt. Airy Forest, Cincinnati's largest park.

Cemetery of Spring Grove, Cincinnati, Ohio

Garden Center of Greater Cleveland

11030 East Blvd.　　　　**(216) 721-1600**
Cleveland, OH 44106

Hours: gardens, every day all hours; building, Mon.–Fri. 9–5, Sun. 2–5, closed Sat., except for special events.
Admission: no fee.
Directions: in the University-Circle section of Cleveland.
Public Transportation: accessible by bus.

The Garden Center of Greater Cleveland, founded in 1930 by members of the Garden Club of Cleveland, is the oldest civic garden center in the U.S. The four-acre site features four distinct gardens: the Herb Garden, maintained by the Western Reserve Herb Society, and considered "one of the largest and most beautiful . . . in the country;" the Rose Garden, planted with both new and old varieties; the Reading Garden, an extension of the library; and the Wick Perennial Borders.

The Chadwick Arboretum

Ohio State University　　　**(614) 422-9775**
2001 Tyffe Court
Columbus, OH 43210

Admission: no fee.
Directions: I–70 to 315 north; right on Lane Ave., then right on Tyffe Rd.

Established on the Ohio State University campus in 1981, the Chadwick Arboretum's 40 acres contain some plant specimens over 100 years old. Major development, including new plantings, is set for 1987 and beyond. Construction of the Arboretum Lake was recently completed.

Cox Arboretum

6733 Springboro Pike　　　**(513) 434-9005**
Dayton, OH 45449

Hours: grounds, every day 8–dusk; offices, Mon.–Fri. 8–4:30, weekends 9–1; shop, Mon.–Fri. 10–4, Sat., 10–2, Sun. 12–3.
Admission: no fee.
Directions: one mi. north of Dayton on Rt. 741 (Springboro Pike).

Public Transportation: accessible by RTA #19 bus.

Cox Arboretum has been developing plant collections on 170 acres since 1964. Managed by the Dayton Montgomery County Park District, the Arboretum was founded in 1962 by James Cox, Jr. Specialized areas include the Rock Garden, Herb Collection and Shrub Garden where examples (emphasizing viburnums) are arranged alphabetically around the South Pond. Other highlights include crabapples, deciduous shade trees (eventually covering 40 acres), evergreens on Conifer Hillside and, in the Woodland, mature specimens of native hardwoods, such as beech, oak, hickory, maple and ash. Floral displays of bulbs, daylilies, hostas, peonies and wildflowers complement the woody collections. The greenhouses (20,000 sq. ft.) shelter ivy (*Hedera helix*), scented geraniums, African violets and succulents.

Stanley M. Rowe Arboretum

4500 Muchmore Rd.   (513) 561-7340
Indian Hill, OH 45243

Hours: dawn–dusk.
Admission: no fee.
Directions: U.S. 50 to Miami Ave. in Mariemont; north on Miami to Muchmore Rd.; right on Muchmore to driveway straight ahead.

The Rowe Arboretum sits on 40 acres that once made up the private estate of Stanley M. Rowe. Started in 1926, it now contains about 900 labeled species. These include extensive collections of crabapples, conifers and lilacs. Other plant groups featured are oaks, magnolias, viburnums, late-summer-blooming trees and shrubs and variegated ornamentals.

Kingwood Center

900 Park Ave. West   (419) 522-0211
Mansfield, OH 44906

Hours: greenhouse and grounds, every day 8–sundown; mansion, Tues.-Sat. 9–5, Sun. (Easter–Oct.) 1:30–4:30.
Admission: no fee.
Directions: I–71 south (from Cleveland) to Rt. 30W exit; left on Trimble Rd., then left on Park Ave. W.; I–71 north (from Columbus) to Rt. 13N exit; left on Cook Rd., right on Trimble Rd. and right on Park Ave. W.

Kingwood Center is 47 acres of formal, informal and "natural" gardens. Spacious lawns, shaded by mature trees and adorned with flower beds, surround Kingwood Hall, the former residence of the late Charles K. King. Formal gardens feature fountains, statuary and clipped hedges. Specialty areas include the Herb, Rose, Perennial, Daylily (testing 300 varieties) and Iris (300 kinds) Gardens. A greenhouse-orangerie complex of six houses (9,000 sq. ft.) offers an indoor light garden, seasonal floral displays and permanent collections of cacti, succulents and orchids.

Charles K. King, one-time president of the Ohio Brass Company of Mansfield, died in 1952, leaving Kingwood with an endowment for its development and maintenance as a public attraction. The Center opened in 1953.

Holden Arboretum

9500 Sperry Rd.   (216) 946-4400
Mentor, OH 44060

Hours: Tues.–Sun. 10–5; closed Dec. 25 and Jan. 1.
Admission: fee charged.
Directions: five mi. southeast of I–90 and Rt. 306 interchange.

The Holden Arboretum, containing over 7,000 accessioned plants on 2,900 acres, is dedicated to woody-plant research and education. More than half of the acreage is an undisturbed nature preserve. Natural habitats include a succession field, young forest, mature woods, oak-hickory, beech-maple and beech-hemlock forests, bog, creek and ravines. Popular collections are the Wildflower Garden, Dogwood and Crabapple Collections, Rhododendron Garden and Lilac Display Garden. Over 20 miles of trails wind among the plantings and natural woodland.

Provision for the Arboretum was originally made in 1912, through a trust set up by Albert Holden.

The Dawes Arboretum

7770 Jacksontown Rd. S.E.   (614) 323-2355
Newark, OH 43055

Hours: every day during daylight; closed Thanksgiving Day, Dec. 25 and Jan. 1.
Admission: no fee.
Directions: five mi. south of Newark on Rt. 13; three mi. north of I–70 (Rt. 13) exit 132; 45 minutes from downtown Columbus.

Of the Dawes Arboretum's 950 acres, the 350 that are open to the public display about 2,000 kinds of woody plants. Designated areas include the Flowering Crabapple Collection, Pine Family Collection, Maples, Oak Collection, Hawthorns, Hollies, Rhododendrons, Azalea Glen, Magnolias, Honey Locusts, Birches, Walnuts, Bald-Cypress Swamp, Dwarf Conifer Collection and Fastigiate Trees.

The Arboretum was founded in 1929 by the Dawes family.

Gardenview Horticultural Park

16711 Pearl Rd. (Rt. 42)   (216) 238-6653
Strongville, OH 44136

Hours: Mar. 1 to Nov. 1, weekends 12–6; groups any time by appointment; open to members at all times.

Admission: fee charged.

Directions: on Rt. 42, 1½ mi. south of Rt. 82; 18 mi. from Cleveland's Public Square.

Six acres of display gardens and a 10-acre arboretum comprise the principal elements of Gardenview Horticultural Park. Established in 1949, Gardenview represents the efforts of its founder, Henry A. Ross. After acquiring 16 acres of vacant land, he worked for the next 14 years developing the gardens. In 1961 he established a foundation to operate the installation.

Gardenview's specialized plantings include: the Spring Garden with tulips, daffodils, azaleas and crabapples; Shade Plants (early spring bulbs and hostas); Rose Gardens; Perennial Beds containing daylilies, iris, peonies and rhododendrons; and two ponds—one for water lilies, the other for waterfowl. Thousands of daffodils and 2,000 flowering and ornamental trees are featured in the Arboretum. Among these, a collection of over 500 varieties of crabapples, some developed by Ross, contributes to a spectacular spring show.

Inniswood Botanical Garden and Nature Preserve

940 Hempstead Rd.   (614) 895-6216
Westerville, OH 43081

Hours: Tues.–Sat. 8–4:30, Sun. 12–5.
Admission: no fee.
Directions: from I–270, exit north towards Westerville, onto Westerville Rd.; right at Schrock Rd. (runs into Inniswood); right at entrance, on Hempstead Rd.

Inniswood, formerly the 37-acre estate of sisters Grace and Mary Innis, became the nucleus of a 91-acre Park District when it was donated by Grace in 1972. Fifty-four acres of woodland were added later.

Major plantings include peonies, bearded iris, daylilies, hostas and naturalized drifts of daffodils. A stone-wall rock garden features alpine plants. Trails lined with wildflowers wind through woodlands.

Secrest Arboretum

Ohio Agricultural Research   (216) 263-3761
and Development Center
Wooster, OH 44619

Hours: every day dawn–dusk.
Admission: no fee.
Directions: one mi. south of Wooster; Hwy. 250 to Ohio Agricultural Research and Development Center; follow Williams Rd. 1 mi. east.

The Secrest Arboretum, a part of the Ohio Agricultural Research and Development Center, is an 85-acre test and display facility for trees and shrubs (2,000 kinds). Features include: the Rhododendron Display Garden, a naturalized planting of azaleas and rhododendrons; flowering crabapples; and native tree and shrub species. In addition, conifers, junipers, arborvitae and forest pines are emphasized. At this writing, more than 140 kinds of trees are being evaluated in the Shade Tree Plot.

The oldest plantings in the Arboretum were set out in 1903. Many of these were made by Edmund Secrest, one-time director of the Research Center, and to whom the Arboretum was dedicated in 1950.

Oklahoma

Will Rogers Horticultural Gardens

3500 NW 36th St.   (405) 943-3977
Oklahoma City, OK 73112

Hours: every day, 8–sunset.
Admission: no fee.
Directions: at the intersection of I–44 and NW 36th St.

The Oklahoma City Parks and Recreation Department operates the Will Rogers Horticultural Gardens, a 17-acre installation founded in 1933. Featured among the Gardens are a collection of daylilies, the Iris Garden (360 varieties) the Rose Garden and the Peony Garden (68 varieties). Woody plantings include the Holly Collection, Native Tree Meadow, redbuds, crape myrtles, the Henry Walter

Philbrook Art Center, Tulsa, Oklahoma

Azalea Trail, ground covers and the Arboretum. Among the 900 species and varieties found in the last "is one of the largest collections of junipers in the country."

Other highlights are: a Memory Garden with plants of yesteryear, a Rock Garden, using the state's native rock, and a Nature Trail through undisturbed countryside. The Conservatory, built in the 1930s, houses orchids and other tropical plants.

Philbrook Art Center

2727 South Rockford Rd.   (918) 749-7941
Tulsa, OK 71114

Hours: grounds, every day 7–5, except legal holidays; Museum, Tues.–Sat. 10–5, Sun 1–5.
Admission: no fee.
Directions: located 3 mi. southeast of downtown Tulsa; I–44 to Peoria St. exit; follow north for 2¼ mi. to 27th Pl.; turn right, one block to Rockford Rd.

Tulsa Garden Center, Inc.

2435 South Peoria St.   (918) 749-6401
Tulsa, OK 74114

Hours: headquarters, weekdays 9–4.
Admission: no fee.
Directions: located in the Woodward Park complex, at 21st and Peoria Sts., near the Utica Square Shopping Center.
Public Transportation: accessible by city bus from downtown.

In 1954 an Italianate mansion (built by an oil baron in 1919) became the Tulsa Garden Center, a meeting place for horticulturists and garden groups. The grounds' ten acres contain a four-acre arboretum, sunken garden and conservatory. Neighboring the Center is Woodward Park, with extensive plantings of azaleas, a rock garden, waterscapes, rustic bridges and test gardens for roses, iris and chrysanthemums.

Oregon

Crystal Springs Rhododendron Garden

SE 28th Ave.   (503) 771-8386
Portland, OR 97202

Hours: every day dawn–dusk.
Admission: no fee.
Directions: located in southeast Portland, adjoining the Eastmoreland Golf Course and adjacent to Reed College.
Public Transportation: accessible by Portland TriMet bus system.

Crystal Springs was started around 1950 by the American Rhododendron Society as a test site for rhododendrons. Today, the Garden displays over 300 rhododendron species, 400 cultivars and companion plants in a woodland setting.

Hoyt Arboretum

4000 SW Fairview Blvd.   (503) 228-8732
Portland, OR 97221

Hours: grounds, every day 6–12; Visitor Center, 10–4.
Admission: no fee.
Directions: from downtown Portland, Hwy. 26W to the Zoo–OMSI exit; follow the main road through the zoo parking lot; right on Fairview Blvd.
Public Transportation: accessible by TriMet Bus #63.

Hoyt Arboretum sits atop a ridge of the Tuality Mountains. Its 200 acres are planted with over 700 species of trees and shrubs (grouped according to botanical family) amid native vegetation. Conifers, including notable redwoods, are represented by 230 species. Oaks, maples and magnolias are other extensive collections. Over ten miles of trails enable visitors to tour while viewing the city and distant mountains.

The Arboretum was established in 1928 when the City of Portland purchased the land on which it was developed.

International Rose Test Garden, Washington Park

400 SW Kingston St.   (503) 796-5193
Portland, OR 97201   248-4302

Hours: every day, 6–12.
Admission: no fee.
Directions: I–5 to the Fremont Bridge to 18th; right at West Burnside, left at Kingston.
Public Transportation: accessible by TriMet Bus #63.

The Japanese Garden

The Japanese Garden	(503) 223-1321
Society of Oregon	223-4070
P.O. Box 3847	
Portland, OR 97208	

Hours: Sept. 16 to Apr. 14, every day 10–4; Apr. 15 to Sept. 15, 10–6; closed Thanksgiving Day, Dec. 25 and Jan 1.
Admission: fee charged.
Directions: located in Washington Park, off Kingston Ave., above the International Rose Test Garden; signs on West Burnside direct the way to the Garden.
Public Transportation: accessible by TriMet Bus #63.

The Japanese Garden, situated on 5 ½ acres, encompasses five distinct gardens: in the Flat Garden; plants, rocks and raked white gravel form a design meant to be viewed from the Japanese-style pavilion veranda; nearby is the Sand and Stone Garden, a rectangular space enclosed by a wall; in the Natural Garden, shallow streams, waterfalls and native plants may be enjoyed from a winding path; the Strolling Pond Garden, the largest in the complex, features waterfalls, ponds, rocks and lush plantings; the Tea Garden contains a teahouse that was brought to Portland from Japan. Along with the various Japanese-design elements, about 400 kinds of plants are on view in these gardens.

Land for The Japanese Garden was set aside in 1961, and soon after, Professor P. T. Tono was selected to execute its design. It opened to the public in 1967.

Pennsylvania

The Henry Foundation for Botanical Research

P.O. Box 7	(215) 525-2037
801 Stony La.	
Gladwyne, PA 19035	

Hours: April–Oct., Tues. and Thurs. 10–4; other times by appointment.
Admission: no fee.
Directions: Schuylkill Expwy. (I–76) west to Gladwyne exit; left off ramp to Rt. 23 (Conshohocken St.); right at 23; after 2 mi. right at Henry La., left at Stony La.; entrance is on right.

The Henry Foundation is dedicated to the collections and preservation of choice American native plants. The 40-acre site contains a rare-plant assemblage that is the result of forty years of travel by Mary G. Henry, the founder of the garden. The plants are grown in naturalized settings amid rock outcroppings. Emphasized collections include *Rhododendron, Styrax, Halesia, Magnolia, Lilium, Vaccinium, Ilex* and *Chionanthus.*

Bowman's Hill Wildflower Preserve, Washington Crossing, Pennsylvania (photo: Professor Al List, Jr.)

Haverford College Arboretum

The Campus	(215) 896-1101
Arboretum Association	
Haverford College	
Haverford, PA 19041	

Hours: every day dawn–dusk.
Admission: no fee.
Directions: from Philadelphia, Schuylkill Expwy. (I–76) west to exit marked Rt. 1 south, City Ave.; after 2 ½ mi., right at Lancaster Ave. (Rt. 30); continue to Haverford; Haverford College is on left, with sign marking entrance.
Public Transportation: accessible by Septa Bus or Paoli Local to Haverford Station.

Hershey Gardens

621 Park Ave.	**(717) 534-3492**
Hershey, PA 17033	

Hours: Apr., May and Sept. through Dec., every day 9–5; Memorial Day through Labor Day, every day 9–7.
Admission: fee charged.
Directions: located in Hershey, adjacent to the Hotel Hershey; Interstate Hwys. 76, 78, 81 and 83 and PA Rts. 322, 422, 39 and 743 lead to Hershey; once there, follow signs to Hotel Hershey and Hershey Gardens.

Hershey Gardens, established in 1936, comprise 23 acres of seasonal flower displays, collections of specimen trees and shrubs, theme gardens and a Rose Garden that contains nearly 14,000 plants of some 800 varieties. These include All-America Selections and some specimens over 45 years old.

Featured collections include hollies, Japanese maples, dwarf and weeping conifers, magnolias and flowering cherries, crabapples, pears and plums.

Longwood Gardens ✕

P.O. Box 501	**(215) 388-6741**
Kennett Square, PA 19348	

Hours: gardens, Apr.–Oct., every day 9–6; Nov.–Mar., every day 9–5; conservatories, every day 10–5; Peirce-du Pont House, Apr.–Nov., every day 11–3.
Admission: fee charged.
Directions: 30 mi. west of Philadelphia on U.S. 1; 12 mi. north of Wilmington, DE (Rt. 52 to U.S. 1); 3 mi. northeast of Kennett Square via U.S. 1.

Longwood Gardens' main fountains and conservatories, Kennett Square, Pennsylvania (photo: Longwood Gardens)

One of America's outstanding horticultural display facilities, Longwood Gardens cover 1,000 acres. Of these, 350 are devoted to outdoor gardens and 3½ are under glass. More than 20 greenhouses are open to the public and some 11,000 kinds of plants are grown indoors and out.

Outstanding features include: the Conservatories—some with changing displays, others with permanent collections: the extravagant fountains, with illuminated evening shows; the outdoor theater; one of the world's largest pipe organs; and the Peirce-du Pont House. Specialty gardens are Flower Garden Walk, Hillside Garden, Italian Water Garden, Topiary Garden, Idea Garden, meadow and collections of bonsai and aquatic plants.

Seasonal displays at Longwood number November's Chrysanthemum Festival, the Christmas show of poinsettias and illuminated trees, and a summer display of waterlilies. Year-round attractions include orchids and roses in the greenhouses, and palms, economic plants, cacti, ferns and tropical pitcher plants in the Conservatories.

The Peirce-du Pont House on the grounds dates back to 1730. Descendants of the Peirce family planted the oldest trees on the property, and the grounds became a local attraction in the 1800s. In 1906 Pierre S. du Pont, who would become chairman of the Du Pont Company and General Motors, purchased the property to save the trees. He started construction of the massive conservatory structures in 1918 and they opened to the public in 1921.

The John J. Tyler Arboretum

P.O. Box 216   (215) 566-9133
Lima, PA 19037

Hours: every day 8–5; longer hours during warm months.
Admission: fee charged.
Directions: I–95 to Rt. 452 west to Barren Rd.; left at Painter Rd.

Two hundred of the 700 acres open to the public at the Tyler Arboretum form a display of woody plants, including trees started in the 1850s. Major collections are the Swarthmore hybrid rhododendrons developed by Dr. John C. Wister, Oriental cherries, crabapples, magnolias, lilacs, dwarf conifers and deciduous shade trees. Other highlights include the native plant trail, fragrant garden and bird-habitat garden. The remaining 500 acres comprise a natural preserve, featuring 20 miles of hiking trails.

The Arboretum was established in 1946 when Laura H. Tyler bequeathed the property in memory of her husband.

Swiss Pines

Charlestown Rd.   (215) 933-6916
R.D. 1, P.O. Box 127
Malvern, PA 19355

Hours: Mon.–Fri. 10–4; Sat. 9–11; closed holidays and Dec. 15–Mar. 15.

Admission: no fee.

Directions: located near the Pennsylvania Tpke. (I–276) overpass at Rt. 29; from Malvern, Rt. 30 onto Rt. 29; under Tpke. overpass, straight ahead on Charlestown Rd.; from Phoenixville, take Nutt Rd.; right at Bridge Rd.; Bridge Rd. becomes Charlestown Rd.

Swiss Pines is best known for the Japanese-style gardens, pavilions and ornaments that occupy much of its 19 acres. The Teahouse and Tea Garden, stone garden, lake, streams, bridges, statuary and stone lanterns, amid naturalistic plantings, all contribute to the Oriental atmosphere.

Specialty plant collections include: the Glendale Azalea Garden (150 kinds); the Herb Garden, designed for low maintenance and containing 100 species; the Ground Cover Garden (28 low-growing plants); and the Pinetum (over 200 kinds of conifers).

Arnold and Meta Bartschi, the originators of Swiss Pines' Japanese design, donated their garden to a foundation in 1960.

Arboretum of the Barnes Foundation

P.O. Box 128   **(215) 664-8880**
Merion Station, PA 19066

Hours: Mon.–Sat. 9:30–4, Sun. 1:30–4; closed holidays.
Admission: no fee.
Directions: Schuylkill Expwy. (I–76) to City Ave. exit; south 2 mi., right at Lapsley La.; from intersection of Rt. 30 and Rt. 1, north 1 mi., left at Lapsley La.
Public Transportation: accessible by train or bus from Philadelphia.

Aside from its primary objective of providing courses for those interested in botany, horticulture and landscape architecture, the Arboretum of the Barnes Foundation offers a diverse collection of woody plants for the enjoyment of the public. These include examples of maples, hollies, oaks, viburnums and lilacs. Other features are a three-acre woodland, a dwarf conifer collection, rose, rock and heath gardens, and the Edgar T. Wherry Memorial Garden.

Bartram's Garden

54th St. and Lindbergh Blvd.   **(215) 729-5281**
Philadelphia, PA 19143

Hours: Garden, every day dawn–dusk; house, May–Oct., every day 10–4, Nov.– Apr., Tues.–Fri. 10–4, closed holidays.
Admission: fee charged for house only.
Directions: I–76 east to University Ave. exit (left); right at Gray's Ferry Ave.; left at Paschall St.; left at 49th St.; bear right onto Gray's Ave.; at next fork, left onto Lindbergh Blvd.; after 54th St., left at Bartram La.
Public Transportation: trolley #36 from City Hall stops at entrance.

Forty-four acres of John Bartram's colonial estate, including the 18th-century stone farmhouse he designed and largely built himself, form the historic site subtitled "America's Oldest Surviving Botanic Garden." As a colon-

ial botanist, Bartram (1699–1777) explored the flora of eastern North America, transplanting discoveries to his own land and shipping specimens across the Atlantic. In this way, he introduced many native American plants to Europe.

Today, on 27 acres open to the public, the Garden displays the plants Bartram collected. Only those grown by him or his son William have been replanted. The house looks out on the Common Flower Garden; to the north stands the stone "Seed House," which Bartram used to store the plants he intended to ship to Europe.

The historic site is administered by the John Bartram Association (founded in 1893 by 400 of his descendants).

Swan Pond, Morris Arboretum, Philadelphia, Pennsylvania

The Horticulture Center

North Horticultural Dr.	**(215) 879-4062**
West Fairmount Park	
Philadelphia, PA 19131	

Hours: Wed.–Sun. 9–3.
Admission: donation requested.
Directions: Schuylkill Expwy (I–76) to Montgomery Dr. exit, travel west; North Horticultural Dr. is the first road to the left.
Public Transportation: bus #38 from center-city Philadelphia.

The Horticulture Center features a 31,000 sq.-ft. greenhouse, seven formal demonstration gardens, the 22-acre Centennial Arboretum and a 13th century-style Japanese House and Garden. The Arboretum contains specimen trees and shrubs, some of which date from the Centennial Exhibition of 1876. The demonstration Gardens provide urban dwellers with ideas for small garden plots. The Japanese House, built in Japan, was added to the site in 1953, and the Garden was installed later by Japanese designers.

Morris Arboretum of the University of Pennsylvania

9414 Meadowbrook Ave.	**(215) 247-5777**
Chestnut Hill	
Philadelphia, PA 19118	

Hours: June–Aug., every day, except Thurs., 10–5; Thurs. (June–Aug.) 10–8; Apr., May, Sept., Oct., every day 10–5; Nov.–Mar., every day 9–4.
Admission: fee charged.
Directions: located in northwest Philadelphia (Chestnut Hill), 5 mi. south of the Pennsylvania Tpke. (I–276).

The Morris Arboretum is a living museum of temperate woody plants, a historical garden, educational institution and research facility affiliated with the University of Pennsylvania. The one-time-private Victorian estate features 3,500 kinds of plants on 90 acres.

Laid out in a naturalistic style amid woodland and pasture, the Arboretum is composed of distinct areas connected by winding paths. Attractions include the Rose Garden (All-America Selections), Formal Parterres, Oriental Gardens, English Park, Azalea Meadow, Magnolia Slope, Oak Allee and Swan Pond. Structures sprinkled throughout the gardens date from the early 1900s. Many rare and notable tree collections include hollies, viburnums, Asian maples, witch hazels, cherries and stewartias.

John T. Morris and his sister Lydia acquired land in Chestnut Hill and began building their estate in 1887. When Lydia died in 1932, she bequeathed the property to the University of Pennsylvania as a public arboretum.

Phipps Conservatory

City of Pittsburgh	**(412) 255-2376**
Schenley Park	
Pittsburgh, PA 15213	

Hours: every day 9–5, also 7–9 p.m during spring and autumn flower shows; closed two days prior to show openings.
Admission: fee charged.
Directions: located on Schenley Dr. in the Oakland section of Pittsburgh, five minutes from the city's downtown area.

Two and half acres of Pittsburgh's Schenley Park lie under the protective glass of the Phipps Conservatory. Winding through the 1893 Victorian structure's 13 connected greenhouses are almost a half mile of walkways. Some of the palms in the central house, the Palm Court, date from 1894 when they were acquired from the Chicago World's Exposition.

Other houses include: the Fern Room, with tree ferns and cycads; the Stove Room, a warm house; the Orchid Room, featuring orchids and bromeliads: the Desert House; the Victoria Room, with waterlilies and tropical trees; the Japanese Room; the Broderie Garden, with a 17th-century French-style embroidery garden; the Economic Room; and several Exhibition Houses featuring changing displays.

The Conservatory came about in 1892 as the result of a gift from steel magnate Henry Phipps. The various substructures, with sloped-glass domes, opened to the public the following year. Ever since they have been operated and maintained by the City's Department of Parks and Recreation.

The Scott Arboretum of Swarthmore College

Swarthmore College   (215) 447-7025
Swarthmore, PA 19081

Hours: offices, Mon.–Fri. 8:30–4:30; grounds, every day sunrise–sunset.
Admission: no fee.
Directions: southwest of Philadelphia; I–95 to Chester, PA, exit; Rt. 320 north about 3 mi.; left at College Ave.; one block to Scott Arboretum.
Public Transportation: SEPTA train (Media local) stops at the campus; bus service from Philadelphia.

The Scott Arboretum, comprising 110 acres of Swarthmore College's landscape, provides a display of ornamental plants best suited to Delaware Valley gardens. Established in 1929 as a living memorial to Arthur Hoyt Scott through a bequest from his family, the Arboretum is made up of more than 5,000 kinds of plants spread throughout the campus. All have been selected for their superior ornamental qualities, ease of maintenance and resistance to disease.

Major collections include: Flowering Cherries, Corylopsis, Crabapples, Lilacs, Magnolias, Rhododendrons, Roses, Tree Peonies, Viburnums and Wisteria. Of special note is the James R. Frorer Holly Collection, with over 220 kinds.

Bowman's Hill Wildflower Preserve

Washington Crossing   (215) 862-2924
Historic Park

Washington Crossing,
PA 18977

Hours: Mon.–Sat. 9–5, Sun. noon–5; buildings closed Jan. 1, Thanksgiving Day and Dec. 25.
Admission: no fee.
Directions: located on River Rd. (Rt. 32), 2½ mi. south of New Hope, PA.

Bowman's Hill Wildflower Preserve, established in 1934, is dedicated to the preservation and conservation of the native flora of Pennsylvania. Within a mile of the Delaware River, the Preserve's 100 acres displays wildflowers, ferns, shrubs, trees and vines in woodland settings along 26 trails. Wildflowers of particular horticultural merit are featured in the Headquarters Garden, and native trees dot Penn's woods, the nine-acre arboretum. Manmade habitats include the pond, sphagnum bog, limestone bluff and serpentine barrens.

Rhode Island

Blithewold Gardens and Arboretum

Ferry Rd.   (401) 253-2707
Bristol, RI 02809

Hours: grounds, every day 10–4; mansion, May 1 to Oct. 31, 10–4, closed Mon. and holidays.
Admission: fee charged.
Directions: 2 mi. south of Bristol, on Rt. 114.
Public Transportation: accessible by bus.

Blithewold Gardens and Arboretum encompass a turn-of-the-century summer residence, with gardens and landscapes typical of the late 19th and early 20th centuries. Overlooking the Narragansett Bay, the 33-acre estate contains about 1,000 kinds of plants. Highlights of the landscape are: the Bosquet, a wooded area filled with ground covers and spring bulbs; the Rock Garden; the Water Garden; the North Garden, featuring blue- and yellow-flowering annuals and perennials; the Cutting Garden; and the Rose Garden.

The Preservation Society of Newport County, Newport, Rhode Island

Planted around 1900, many of the Arboretum's woody specimens are notably mature. These include Chinese cedar, ginkgo, Japanese tree lilac and a grove of bamboo. Blithewold also boasts the largest giant sequoia (80 ft. tall) east of the Rockies.

The Gardens, largely completed by 1895, were designed by John Dewolf. Originally owned by coal magnate Augustus Van Winkle, the estate was eventually inherited by his daughter Marjorie. When she died in 1976, Blithewold became the property of the Heritage Foundation of Rhode Island.

Green Animals

Location Address:	**Mailing Address:**
Cory's La.	The Preservation Society
Portsmouth, RI	of Newport County
(401) 683-1267	118 Mill St.

Newport, RI 02840
(401) 847-1000

Hours: May–Sept., every day 10–5; Oct., weekends 10–5; holidays 10–5; at other times, groups of 20 or more (reservations required).
Admission: fee charged; combination tickets for the Newport Mansions (see previous entry) include Green Animals.
Directions: located on Cory's La. off Rt. 114, 0.3 mi. from the intersection of 114 and 24; next to St. Philomena's School and across from Portsmouth Abbey and School.

Green Animals is noted for its 80 animal-shaped topiaries. The seven-acre estate also includes: annual, perennial and rose beds in geometric patterns; fruits trees; herb garden; dahlia garden; vegetable garden; espaliered fruit trees; magnolias; gourd and grape arbors; cold frames; and greenhouses. In the Formal Garden, geometric shapes are fashioned from California privet, golden boxwood, yew and

American boxwood. The menagerie of topiary animals includes a bear, boar, camel, dogs, donkey, elephant, giraffe, horse, lion, goat, ostrich, peacocks, rooster and swan.

The estate was bequeathed to The Preservation Society of Newport County in 1972.

Newport Mansions

The Preservation Society   **(401) 847-1000**
of Newport County
118 Mill St.
Newport, RI 02840

Hours: vary with each mansion; call for information.
Admission: varies with each mansion; a variety of reduced-rate combination tickets are available; for reservations, call 847-6543.
Directions: located in the Bellevue area of Newport.

A group of lavishly constructed mansions sited along the Atlantic coastline are jointly operated and maintained by the Preservation Society of Newport County. The structures span a time period of 1748 to 1902 and are notable for the magnificence of their mature plant specimens.

Wilcox Park

17½ High St.   **(401) 348-8362**
Westerly, RI 02891

Hours: every day, all times.
Admission: no fee.
Directions: Rt. 1 into Westerly; Park is in the heart of the village.

Wilcox Park, designed by Warren H. Manning, former associate of Frederick Law Olmsted, was established in 1898. Plants native to the region dominate its gardens, but in the 1960s efforts were begun toward the development of the Park as an arboretum, and new installations were made accordingly. Specialty areas include the Dwarf Conifer

Garden (in a rock-strewn setting), Herb Garden, Garden of the Senses and Perennial Garden. Wilcox also contains examples (a fountain, lily pond and bandstand) of the fine granite work for which the region was once known. The Park was placed on the National Register of Historic Places in 1973.

South Carolina

Magnolia Plantation and Gardens

Rt. 4, Hwy. 61   **(803) 571-1266**
Charleston, SC 29407

Hours: every day 8–6; closed Dec. 25.
Admission: fee charged.
Directions: located on Hwy. 61, 10 mi. south of Charleston; 14 mi. from Summerville.

Magnolia Plantation and Gardens, on the National Register of Historic Places, began in the late 1600s as an estate plantation. Reaching an exceptional degree of maturity in the years since, its 50 acres of gardens feature masses of azaleas, camellias (over 500) and magnolias under a canopy of live oaks and cypress. Bounded by the Ashley River, the 500-acre property is owned and operated by ninth-generation descendants of its original owners.

Plantings in relatively recent years include the 18th century-style herb garden and 17th century-style maze. Bordering the Gardens and cutting through the 125-acre waterfowl refuge are five miles of nature trails.

Middleton Place

Ashley River Rd.   **(803) 556-6020**
Charleston, SC 29407

Hours: grounds, every day 9–5; House, closed Mon. mornings and two weeks in mid-winter.
Admission: fee charged.
Directions: located 14 mi. northwest of

Charleston on Hwy. 61 (Ashley River Rd.).

Middleton Place, a National Historic Landmark, boasts the oldest landscaped garden (laid out by Henry Middleton in 1741) extant in America. Surrounding the restored Middleton Place House (built in 1755) and the Plantation Stableyards, the 100 acres of the garden open to the public feature over 200 kinds of plants, as well as numerous farm animals.

In the late 18th century, Andre Michaux planted America's first camellias at Middleton Place, and many of these can still be seen today; later additions form flowering canopies during the winter months. Massive live oaks, including the famous Middleton Oak (estimated to be several hundred years old), over 35,000 azaleas, southern magnolias and some of the largest crape myrtles in the country are other attractions.

The Middleton Place Foundation governs the historic site.

Brookgreen Gardens' Live Oak Allé, Murrells Inlet, South Carolina

Park Seed Company Gardens

Hwy. 254 North   (803) 374-3341
Greenwood, SC 29647

Hours: Mon.–Fri. 8–4:30; closed holidays.
Admission: no fee.
Directions: located 0.5 mi. north of Greenwood on Hwy. 254 North.

The Park Seed Company Gardens constitute the largest trial garden for annuals in the

southeast. On the five acres of the test and research facility open to the public, 500 kinds of spring bulbs and 1,500 to 2,000 varieties of summer annuals and perennials may be seen and compared. The Company was founded in 1868 by George W. Park.

Magnolia Plantation and Gardens, Charleston, South Carolina

Brookgreen Gardens

Hwy. 17 South   (803) 237-4218
Murrells Inlet, SC 29576

Hours: every day 9:30–4:45; closed Dec. 25.
Admission: fee charged.
Directions: 17 mi. south of Myrtle Beach, 17 mi. north of Georgetown, on U.S. Hwy. 17.

Over 400 pieces of American 19th- and 20th-century sculpture are set among tranquil gardens, fountains, courtyards, allées, ponds and woodland at Brookgreen Gardens. On the 300 acres that form the Gardens proper, horticultural highlights include: the Dogwood Garden, divided into four quadrants, each with a pool; the Small Sculpture Gallery, enclosed in the manner of a cloister garden; the South Carolina Terrace: the Live Oak and Magnolia Allées; the Diana Pool; the Palmetto Garden, also with a reflecting pool; the Fountain of the Muses Garden, with pergolas and raised planting beds; the Arboretum; and Dogwood, Opuntia and Cypress Ponds. In direct contrast to the manicured formality of the

Memphis Botanic Garden, Japanese Garden, Memphis, Tennessee

sculpture gardens is Brookgreen's 50-acre wildlife park, with animals and native plants.

The Gardens were started—with the intent of sharing them with the public—by Mr. and Mrs. Archer M. Huntington in 1931. Brookgreen Gardens, Inc., A Society for Southeastern Flora and Fauna, was organized, and today the corporation administers the Gardens, wildlife park and collections.

Tennessee

Reflection Riding

Garden Rd. (Rt. 4)   (615) 821-1160
Chattanooga, TN 37409

Hours: every day during daylight, except Sun. mornings.
Admission: fee charged.
Directions: located southwest of Chattanooga; turn south off Cummings Hwy. (U.S. 41) ¼ mi. west of Lookout Mountain; go 1 mi. on Garden Rd. (Rt.4).

Reflection Riding is a 300-acre nature preserve, with a variety of native trees and shrubs, that may be enjoyed from numerous walking trails or over three miles of automobile roadway.

Mr. and Mrs. John Chambliss established

Reflection Riding in 1956.

The Dixon Gallery and Gardens

4339 Park Ave.   (901) 761-2409
Memphis, TN 38117

Hours: Tues.–Sat. 11–5, Sun. 1–5; closed Jan. 1, July 4, Labor Day, Thanksgiving Day, Dec. 24, 25 and 31.
Admission: fee charged, except on Tues.
Directions: located 9 mi. east of downtown Memphis; I–240 to Getwell exit north; right at Park Ave.; on the right within 1 mi.

An attraction for art and plant lovers alike, the Dixon Gallery and Gardens, open to the public since 1976, offer 17 landscaped acres and a collection of impressionist paintings. Margaret and Hugo Dixon began developing the estate in 1940. With the assistance of Mr. Dixon's sister, noted landscape architect Hope Crutchfield, and utilizing French cross-axis design, the Dixons created a garden reminiscent of English park settings. Vistas emphasize mature oaks, and walks feature ground covers, herbaceous plants and garden statuary.

Memphis Botanic Garden

750 Cherry Rd. (901) 685-1566
Memphis, TN 38117

Hours: grounds and gardens, every day 8–sundown; Goldsmith Civic Garden Center, Mon.–Fri. 9–5, weekends 1–5; closed major holidays.
Admission: no fee.
Directions: located in Audubon Park in east Memphis; near I–240 and Memphis State University.
Public Transportation: accessible by Memphis Area Transit Authority bus.

In the southeastern corner of Audubon Park (373 acres) are 120 acres that form the Memphis Botanic Garden. Over 2,000 kinds of plants may be found in its collections. Begun in 1953, the Garden is operated by the Memphis Park Commission.

Among the 15 specialized areas offered are: the Iris Garden, containing several hundred varieties on five acres; the Dahlia Garden; the Daylily Trial Garden; the Magnolia Garden, started in 1958, with many exotic species; the Conifer Garden; the Rose Garden, with 4,000 plants; the Wildflower Garden—over 300 species and varieties in a naturally wooded cove; the Azalea and Dogwood Trail, planted amid an oak forest; the Daffodil Trail; the Test Garden, where plants from the U.S.D.A. are observed; the Japanese Garden, surrounding Lake Biwa; the Cactus Garden; and the Perennial Garden.

Plants indigenous to the mid-South are emphasized in the woody collections, and the 3,000 sq.-ft. conservatory displays about 500 kinds of tropicals.

Tennessee Botanical Gardens and Fine Arts Center at Cheekwood

Forrest Park Dr. (615) 352-5310
Nashville, TN 37205

Hours: Tues.–Sat. 9–5, Sun 1–5; closed Thanksgiving Day, Dec. 24, 25, 31 and Jan. 1.

Admission: fee charged.

Directions: located 8 mi. southwest of downtown Nashville; Broadway/West End Ave./Harding Rd. to Belle Meade Blvd.; left at Belle Meade; right at Page Rd.; left at Forrest Park Dr.; Cheekwood is at the top of Forrest Park Dr., on the right.

Public Transportation: two buses (Metropolitan Transit Authority) leave downtown Nashville to Belle Meade-Cheekwood daily; call (615) 352-5310.

Once the residence of Mr. and Mrs. Leslie Cheek, Cheekwood (built between 1929 and 1932) today functions as a display garden and fine arts center. Its 18th-century Georgian-style mansion and English-style landscape were designed by Bryant Fleming. In 1959 the Cheeks' daughter gave the 55-acre estate to a not-for-profit organization to maintain it as a cultural center for Nashville and the mid-South. It was opened to the public in 1960.

An ingenious system of artificial brooks, ponds, recycling fountains, cascading waterfalls and a collection of boxwood are survivors of the original landscaping. Several plant collections and gardens have been added to Cheekwood in the years since it became a public attraction: The Wills Garden, dedicated in 1981, displays iris and other perennials along winding paths; "Wildings," once the wildflower garden of Mrs. H.A. Howe, was transplanted to Cheekwood after her death in 1967; in the three circular areas of Burr Garden, roses, herbs and perennials are emphasized. A path through this section is bordered by 1,600 azaleas.

Other highlights include the Daffodil Garden, Herb Study Garden and Mustard Meadow, where the mustard indigenous to Nashville forms a yellow carpet in early April. Four greenhouses (5,000 sq. ft.) display orchids, camellias and, in the Cloud Forest Greenhouse, "a little piece of Central America"—bromeliads, other epiphytes and plants native to Central America re-creating a tropical environment.

University of Tennessee Arboretum

901 Kerr Hollow Rd.   **(615) 483-3571**
Oak Ridge, TN 37830

Hours: grounds, every day 8–sunset; office, Mon.–Fri. 8–5.
Admission: no fee.
Directions: located 20 mi. west of Knoxville, 3 mi. south of Oak Ridge Tpke. (Rt. 61) on Rt. 62 (Kerr Hollow Rd.).

Two hundred and fifty of the 2,260 acres that make up the Tennessee Arboretum are open to the public. Woody collections include pines, magnolias, dogwoods and willows. The Arboretum serves as an official test facility for hollies, and boasts many rare and unusual dwarf conifers. In all, more than 700 kinds of trees and shrubs may be seen via a system of trails and roads.

Specialty areas include models of California, Southern Coastal Plain, Central China and Heather Forests, experimental plant screens and shade trees, a marsh and reflecting pond for moisture-loving plants.

The Arboretum was started in 1964 as a project of the Forestry Department.

Texas

Dallas Arboretum and Botanical Garden

8525 Garland Rd.	Business Office:
Dallas, TX 75218	8617 Garland Rd.
(214) 327-8263	Dallas, TX 75218
	(214) 327-8263

Hours: gardens, Tues.–Sun. 10–6; DeGolyer House, Tues.–Fri. 10–4.
Admission: fee charged; no fee on Tues.
Directions: located in east Dallas on White Rock Lake; Garland Rd. is between I–635 and I–30.

Tennessee Botanical Gardens and Fine Arts Center at Cheekwood, Nashville, Tennessee

Public Transportation: accessible by city buses.

The Dallas Arboretum and Botanical Society is working on a master plan for two adjoining sites along White Rock Lake: the 22-acre Camp Estate and the 44-acre DeGolyer property. Under development is a collection of Texas trees, shrubs, vines and flowers, as well as plants native to the southwestern U.S. and other countries. The former estates have been graced with trails, walks, floral displays and testing/demonstration gardens. Restoration of the historic DeGolyer gardens began in 1985, and major renovation is underway.

The Dallas Arboretum and Botanical Society founded DABG in 1970.

Dallas Garden Center

P.O. Box 26194   (214) 428-7476
Dallas, TX 75226

Hours: Mon.–Fri. 10–5, weekends 9–5; closed Dec. 24, 25 and Jan. 1.
Admission: no fee.
Directions: located on Martin Luther King Ave. in the southwest corner of the State Fairgrounds; I–30 to Second Ave. exit, just south of downtown Dallas.
Public Transportation: accessible from downtown by city bus (ten-minute ride).

A series of small outdoor gardens and a 6,884 sq.-ft. conservatory complex constitute the Dallas Garden Center's seven and a half acres. The multilevel outdoor areas include: the Callier Garden, with a fountain as its focus; the All-America Garden—colorful annuals in a geometric design; the Herbert Marcus Senior Garden, with a large turn-of-the-century Italian urn; the Josson Garden, featuring water and live oaks; the Shakespeare Garden; and the Herb and Scent Garden.

The contemporary conservatory complex houses about 450 varieties of tropical plants, including orchids and over 90 species of bromeliads. A free-standing waterfall provides gurgling sounds, and visitors may view the entire Tropical Room from a 16 ft.-high catwalk.

Fort Worth Botanic Garden

3220 Botanic Garden Dr.   (817) 870-7686
Fort Worth, TX 76107

Hours: every day 8–11; Japanese Garden, Apr.–Oct., Tues.–Sat. 9–7, Sun. 1–7; Nov.–Mar., Tues.–Sat. 10–5, Sun.1–5; production greenhouses, Mon.–Fri. 8–3:45
Admission: fee charged for Japanese Garden only.
Directions: from the intersection of I–30 and I–35, travel west on I–30; left at University Dr. north exit; left at Botanic Garden Dr.
Public Transportation: accessible by city bus.

Construction of the Fort Worth Botanic Garden, underwritten with Federal Relief Funds, began in 1933 on 37 acres. Since then, its size has expanded to 114 acres, with over 2,000 kinds of plants in a variety of formal and informal settings.

Gardens include: the Rose Garden, with 3,500 plants; the Fragrance Garden; the Test Garden (All-America Selections of annuals and roses); and the seven-acre Japanese Garden, installed in the 1970s with a variety of gates, teahouses and pavilions. Other areas of interest are the arboretum, displaying over 150 kinds of trees, the cactus garden and the water garden, a series of lagoons at the site of the original Rock Springs. Informal plantings of azaleas and beds of annuals and perennials provide seasonal color. The Exhibition Greenhouse, adjoining the Garden Center, is filled with tropicals.

Fort Worth Water Gardens

Parks and   (817) 870-7699
Recreation Department
1501 Commerce St.
Fort Worth, TX 76102

Hours: fountains run every day 12 noon to 10:30 p.m.
Admission: no fee.
Directions: located west of I–35W and

north of I–30 (East-West Frwy.) in down-town Fort Worth.

Five fountain "sculptures," in which enormous amounts of water cascade to depths 16 to 38 ft. below street level, make up this unique urban installation. Covering 4.3 acres and completed in 1974 at a cost of $7 million, the "Gardens" were a gift of the Amon G. Carter Foundation. Five hundred coastal live oak, sweet gum, bald cypress, pistachio and white wisteria trees, plus a grove of ginkgos, accent the concrete, earth and water of the design, and ground covers contribute texture and color. The award-winning Gardens were conceived by architect Philip Johnson and John Burgee.

San Antonio Botanical Center

555 Funston Pl.	(512) 821-5115
San Antonio, TX 78209	

Hours: Tues.–Sun. 9–6; closed Dec. 25.
Admission: fee charged.
Directions: located in San Antonio, two blocks off Broadway on Funston Pl., between Brackenbridge Park and Ft. Sam Houston.
Public Transportation: via Transit to Broadway (two blocks to Funston).

The San Antonio Botanical Center opened to the public in 1980. The 33-acre site displays about 4,500 kinds of plants. A series of formal gardens includes the Old-Fashioned Garden (annuals and perennials), Herb Garden, with herbs used by Texas settlers, Biblical Garden and Rose Garden. Other points of interest are the Garden for the Blind and the Gazebo-Observatory, offering a panorama of the plantings.

Representations of three of Texas' unique ecological sectors, including plants and historic structures, are featured attractions at the Center. The East Texas Area, encompassing the Nacogdoches-Lufkin region, contains 1,300 native plants and three log buildings characteristic of the late 1800s. Two adobe structures and 900 different plants (cacti, yucca, live

oaks) suggest Southwest Texas. The Hill Country/Edwards Plateau Native Area is a rolling meadow planted with 1,100 kinds of wildflowers, trees and shrubs.

Utah

State Arboretum of Utah

University of Utah	(801) 581-5322
Building 436	
Salt Lake City, UT 84112	

Hours: campus grounds, every day all hours; Arboretum Office, Mon.–Fri. 8–5; Conservatory, by appointment only; Red Butte Development Site, Apr.–Oct., Mon.–Fri. 8–5.
Admission: no fee.
Directions: located on the University of Utah campus, 3 mi. from downtown Salt

State Arboretum of Utah, Salt Lake City, Utah

Lake City; at the intersection of 100 South and 1400 East.

Public Transportation: accessible from downtown Salt Lake City by Utah Transit Authority buses #4, #24 and #11.

The 1,500-acre campus of the University of Utah forms a major portion of the State Arboretum of Utah, established in 1961. On land gradually reclaimed from the Utah sagebrush steppe since 1930, the Arboretum is now forested with over 8,000 trees of 300 species and varieties. Over 400 exotic taxa are represented in the Conservatory (1,100 sq. ft.). The Red Butte Development Site, encompassing an additional 147 acres, harbors more than 300 large conifers and an extensive collection (over 75 taxa) of dwarf kinds.

Specialized areas on the University grounds include the Cottam Hybrid Oak Grove, the conifer collection (over 40 taxa) and the Faculty Women's Club Rose Garden. The Arboretum boasts the largest Russian Olive (*Elaegnus angustifolia*) in the United States.

Vermont

Shelburne Museum and Heritage Park

Shelburne, VT 05482   (802) 985-3344

Hours: mid-May through late Oct., every day 9–5; Sun. in winter, 11–4.
Admission: fee charged.
Directions: located 7 mi. south of Burlington, on U.S. 7.
Public Transportation: accessible from Burlington by bus.

The 45-acre Shelburne Museum features over 35 historic exhibit buildings in a parklike setting. Specialty plantings include the Herb, Rock and Rose Gardens. The collection of Americana displayed indoors ranges from waterfowl decoys to circus figurines. The Museum was founded in 1947 by Electra Havemeyer Webb to "show the craftsmanship of our forefathers."

Virginia

American Horticultural Society: River Farm

Location:	Mailing Address:
7931 East Boulevard Dr.	P.O. Box 0105
Alexandria, VA	Mount Vernon, VA
22308	2212

Hours: Mon.–Fri. 8:30–5
Admission: no fee.
Directions: located 4 mi. south of Alexandria, on George Washington Pkwy.; left at "East Boulevard Dr., Herbert Springs Arcturus" sign, and follow signs.

River Farm, one of the five farms that once formed George Washington's Mount Vernon estate, is the home of the American Horticultural Society (AHS). The 25 acres of gently rolling hills, river frontage, lawns and large shade trees (admired by Washington) now provide Society members and visitors with various test and display gardens.

Plantings of boxwood, magnolias, wisteria and other ornamentals set off the main house. In addition to its historical attractions, River Farm features modern plants in its idea garden and in its All-America Selections (roses, annuals, vegetables) gardens. Daylilies, lilies, marigolds, iris, chrysanthemums, cacti and succulents are also featured, and the site is an official test facility for dahlias. Additional specialized areas include a demonstration orchard, children's garden, herb garden, meadow and water garden.

Woodlawn Plantation

Location:	(703) 557-7880
900 Richmond Hwy	(703) 557-7881
Alexandria, VA	Mailing Address:
	P.O. Box 37
	Mount Vernon, VA 22121

Hours: every day 9:30–4:30; closed Thanksgiving Day, Dec. 25 and Jan. 1.
Admission: fee charged.
Directions: located 14 mi. south of Washington, D.C., on U.S. 1; 3 mi. west

of Mount Vernon.
Public Transportation: accessible by
Washington Metro Bus.

**Blandy Experimental Farm and
Orland E. White Research Arboretum**

University of Virginia   (703) 837-1758
P.O. Box 175
Boyce, VA 22620

Hours: every day, sunrise–sunset.
Admission: no fee.
Directions: located 1.5 mi. east of the junctions of Rts. 17, 50 and 340, 4 mi. west of the Shenandoah River Bridge across Rts. 17 and 50; entrance is on Rts. 17 and 50.

The Blandy Experimental Farm is the result of a gift of 700 acres from Graham F. Blandy to the University of Virginia in 1926. Under the Farm's first director, Dr. Orland White, a number of trees and shrubs were brought to it for observation and research, and a 100-acre Arboretum was the eventual outcome. Today, more than 1,000 kinds of plants grow at the research facility.

The Orland E. White Arboretum specializes in boxwood (headquarters of the American Boxwood Society) and conifers, and features an extensive planting of ginkgos and an herb garden. Other specialties include magnolias, maples, oak, roses and olives.

Ash Lawn

Rt. 6, P.O. Box 37   (804) 293-9539
Charlottesville, VA 22901

Hours: Mar.–Oct., every day 9–6; Nov.–Feb., 10–5; closes Thanksgiving Day, Dec. 25 and Jan. 1.
Admission: fee charged.
Directions: located 5 mi. southeast of Charlottesville's city limits, 2½ mi. past Monticello.

Ash Lawn, a historic house/museum, was the home of James Monroe, the fifth President of the United States. The 535-acre site is owned and operated by the College of William and Mary, and 20 acres are open to the public. Plants popular during Monroe's lifetime are featured in the vicinity of the house and

Mount Vernon Ladies Association, Mount Vernon, Virginia

throughout the landscape. A vegetable garden and an herb garden are other highlights.

Monticello

P.O. Box 316	(804) 295-8181
Charlottesville, VA 22902	(804) 295-2657

Hours: Mar.–Oct., every day 8–5; Nov.–Feb., 9–4:30; closed Dec. 25.
Admission: fee charged.
Directions: located 1.5 mi. southeast of Charlottesville, on Rt. 53.

At Monticello, Thomas Jefferson's personality is reflected in the house he designed and in the gardens and grounds he developed so carefully for more than 40 years. About the property, he laid out terraces, lawns, a "roundabout" walk bordered by flower beds, an extensive (1,000 ft.–long) vegetable garden, orchards and vineyards, in addition to the numerous outbuildings necessary for the functioning of a farm. Through archaeological investigation and referral to Jefferson's Garden Book, much of the site has been restored according to his plan. Today, Monticello's plantings feature over 150 cultivated species of pre-1826 annuals and perennials, vegetables grown in the 19th century and species native to Virginia.

Mount Vernon

Mount Vernon	(703) 780-2000
Ladies' Association	
Mount Vernon, VA 22121	

Hours: Apr.–Oct., every day 9–5; Nov.–Mar., 9–4.
Admission: fee charged, except on George Washington's Birthday.
Directions: located at the southern terminus of Mount Vernon Memorial Hwy., 8 mi. south of Alexandria and 16 mi. from downtown Washington, D.C.

Public Transportation: accessible by tour bus and boat cruises from Washington.

Mount Vernon, the former home of George Washington, is owned and operated by the Mount Vernon Ladies' Association, founded in 1853. About 30 of the estate's 500 acres are open to the public, and these are presented as they might have appeared in 1799, the year of Washington's death.

Some of the mature trees bordering the bowling green at the entrance to the property date from the original planting. On opposite sides of this large expanse of lawn are the wall-enclosed Kitchen Garden and the Flower Garden. The boxwood-edged beds of the latter are planted with flowers that were familiar to 18th-century Virginians. Between the Flower Garden and mid-Georgian manor house is the Botanical Garden, where Washington experimented with various plant materials.

Norfolk Botanical Gardens

Norfolk VA 23518	(804) 853-6972

Hours: Gardens, every day 8:30–sunset; administration buildings, Mon.–Fri. 8:30–5, weekends and holidays 10–5.
Admission: fee charged, except Christmas week.
Directions: from Norfolk, follow signs for the International Airport; located north of the Airport, bordered by Rt. 170.

The Norfolk Botanical Gardens cover 175 acres and feature extensive azalea and camellia plantings. Over 12 miles of pathways lead visitors through a setting of native plants, 250,000 azaleas and over 700 varieties of camellias. Containing 4,500 kinds of plants in all, the Gardens are just inland from Chesapeake Bay and are operated by the City of Norfolk's Department of Parks and Recreation.

Features include: the New Rose Garden, with over 4,000 roses of 250 varieties, fountains, terraces and sculpture; the Japanese Garden; Sanctuary Vista, graced with 11 Victorian-style statues; the Fragrance Garden; Holly Garden; Lone Pine Garden; Colonial Garden; Figure Eight Garden; Ferndale Enchanted Forest; Conifers; Desert Garden; Renaissance Garden; Flowering Arboretum, with over 400 trees; Perennial Vista; and a 2,550 sq.-ft. greenhouse, displaying orchids year-round. Containing an All-America test garden for annuals and roses, the Gardens grow over 40,000 annuals each year. Visitors may view the entire Gardens from the Observation Tower.

Norfolk Botanical Gardens were established in 1938 as a WPA (Work Projects Administration) undertaking.

Maymont

1700 Hampton St.	(804) 358-7166
Richmond, VA 23220	

Hours: grounds, Apr.–Oct., every day 10–7, Nov.–Mar. 10–5; indoor exhibits, Apr.–Oct., Tues.–Sun. 12–5, Nov.–Mar., 12–4, closed Thanksgiving Day, Dec. 25 and Jan. 1.
Admission: no fee.
Directions: I–95 to Exit 14 south; travel 2 mi., then follow Maymont signs to Hampton St. entrance.

Maymont, a 105-acre estate operated as a family park by the Maymont Foundation, was once the home of Major and Mrs. James Henry Dooley. It was bequeathed to the City of Richmond in 1925, and declared a National Historic Landmark in 1971. Five hundred kinds of plants are incorporated into the landscape and gardens.

The house is a neo-Romanesque residence, typical of the Gilded Age. Horticultural attractions include a formal Italian Garden, Japanese Garden, Arboretum, Herb Garden and Wildflower Garden. The Renaissance-style Italian Garden features fountains, a water cascade, pergola and elaborate stonework. A 75-ft. waterfall, streams, arched bridges, stones and appropriate plants are combined in the four-acre Japanese Garden. The trees in the Arboretum and on the grounds total 1,000, and many of them have been designated State Champions.

Colonial Williamsburg

P.O. Box Drawer C	(804) 229-1000
Williamsburg, WA 23187	

Hours: Mar.–Nov., plus the last two weeks in Dec. (including Dec. 25), every day 9–5; walking tours of the gardens, Mon.–Fri. 10:30–2:30.
Admission: fee charged.
Directions: I–64E from Richmond (1 hour); I–64W from Norfolk (45 minutes); historic buildings and gardens line Duke of Gloucester St.

Numerous gardens surround the re-created and restored buildings that comprise historic Colonial Williamsburg. The designs of the gardens are based on several sources: maps of the old town, remnants of Virginia's colonial plantations and British gardens that date from the time of King William III, for whom Williamsburg was named. Today, nearly 100 acres of the restoration are either gardens or "greens."

The most extensive garden graces the Governor's Palace; it features English, French and Dutch styles of landscape design. In addition to touring the Palace grounds, visitors may spend a day discovering the many smaller, more intimate gardens, featuring topiary, herbs, vegetables and native and exotic ornamentals.

Restoration of Colonial Williamsburg as an "outdoor museum" began in 1926, with the support of Mr. and Mrs. John D. Rockefeller.

Washington

Bloedel Reserve

7571 N.E. Dolphin Dr.	(206) 842-7631
Brainbridge Island, WA 98110	

Hours: for groups (10 to 50 people) only, by appointment.
Admission: no fee.
Directions: phone for directions and appointment.

Seymour Conservatory, Tacoma, Washington

Rhododendron Species Foundation

P.O. Box 3798   (206) 927-6960
Federal Way, WA 98063-3798   838-4646

Hours: mid–Mar. to May, Wed. 10–3, Sun. 1–5; for Fall Foliage Festival, mid-Oct., 10–5 (call for exact dates, which change yearly); year-round, Mon.–Fri. 10–3, by appointment.
Admission: fee charged.
Directions: located 24 mi. south of Seattle on I–5; Hwy. 18 to Exit 142A east; left (north) at 32nd Ave. South; continue to the entrance of Weyerhaeuser Corporate Headquarters; located on the southwest corner of the Weyerhaeuser campus.

The Rhododendron Species Foundation (RSF) was formed in 1964, and the present 24-acre display garden began development in 1974. The Weyerhaeuser Company offered the land on a long-term lease, and provided partial funding. Over 10,000 rhododendrons representing more than 500 species have been collected by the RSF. The garden constitutes one of the "most diverse and complete collections of species rhododendrons in the world."

Rhododendrons from all parts of the globe are represented at RSF. In the Study Garden, selected plants are grouped to indicate their botanical relationships. Specialized habitats include a meadow, pond area and alpine area.

Carl S. English, Jr., Gardens

Army Corps of Engineers   (206) 783-7059
3015 NW 54th St.
Seattle, WA 98107

Hours: gardens, every day 8–9; Visitor Center, summer, every day 11–9, winter, Thurs.–Mon. 11–5.
Admission: no fee.
Directions: I–5 to NE 45th St. exit west; travel about 6 mi.
Public Transportation: Metropolitan Bus Authority, Rts. 43 and 17.

The Carl S. English, Jr., Gardens contain about 800 species of native and exotic plants, with trees and shrubs emphasized. Special collections include rhododendrons, pines, oaks and magnolias.

The Gardens, located at Chittenden navigational locks, were developed by Carl S. English, Jr., who, from 1933 to 1974, gathered plants from all over the world.

Washington Park Arboretum

University of Washington   (206) 543-8800
(XD-10)
Seattle, WA 98195

Hours: every day 8–sunset; Japanese Garden, Mar.–Nov. only.

Admission: Arboretum, no fee; Japanese Garden, fee charged.
Directions: located between Montlake Blvd. and E. Madison on Lake Washington Blvd. East; from I–5, take Exit 168 (Bellevue-Kirkland), then take the first exit (Montlake-University of Washington); at the light, cross Montlake Blvd. to Lake Washington Blvd.; at stop sign, turn left onto Foster Island Rd., and follow signs to the office.
Public Transportation: accessible by Metro bus #11, 43, 48 from all parts of the city.

The Washington Park Arboretum, affiliated with the Center for Urban Horticulture of the University of Washington, displays about 5,500 species of woody plants on 200 acres. At the northern end of the site is Foster's Island, where alders, birches, pines and oaks are planted in a natural setting. Other highlights include: the Winter Garden; the Woodland Garden, with two ponds and a creek surrounded by a collection of Japanese maples (planted in 1940); Loderi Valley, a wooded area planted with magnolias and hybrids of *Rhododendron loderi;* Rhododendron Glen; and Azalea Way, the Arboretum's major trail, lined with flowering cherries, azaleas and dogwoods. At the southern end of the site is the Japanese Garden, displaying Oriental-style plantings in a pond setting. Other plant groups to be found on the grounds include conifers, Legume Family members, mountain ashes, camellias, cistus and lindens.

Originally Washington Park, Washington Park Arboretum began devoting itself to the preservation and display of trees and shrubs in 1924.

Woodland Park Zoological Gardens

5500 Phinney Ave. North   (206) 782-1265
Seattle, WA 98103

Hours: winter months, every day 8:30–4; summer months, 8:30–6.
Admission: fee charged.
Directions: located 2 mi. west of I–5 on North 50th St.; 6 mi. north of downtown

Seattle; near Green Lake, just off U.S. 99 (Aurora Ave.).
Public Transportation: accessible by Bus #5 from downtown Seattle.

The Woodland Park Zoological Gardens provide simulated native habitats for some 400 species of animals. Woodland Park, originally a private estate developed in the late 1800s, was laid out in traditional English-park style. A formal rose garden, with All-America Selections and topiaries, and about 3,000 stately old trees remain from the early years.

Seymour Conservatory

Wright Park   (206) 591-5330
South I and G Sts.
Tacoma, WA 98407

Hours: every day 8–4:20
Admission: no fee.
Directions: I–5 into Tacoma to City Center off ramp; right at Pacific Ave.; left at City Hall; first right, then first left onto 3rd St.; four blocks to Wright Park.
Public Transportation: accessible by Metro Bus.

Seymour Conservatory is located in Tacoma's one-acre Wright Park. The Victorian structure—built in 1908, fully restored in 1975-76 and designated a Historic Landmark —shelters palms, ferns and other tropicals under its glass dome.

Ohme Gardens

3327 Ohme Rd.   (509) 662-5785
Wenatchee, WA 98801

Hours: Apr. 15 to Oct. 15, every day 9–dusk.
Admission: fee charged.
Directions: located 3 mi. north of Wenatchee, near the junction of Hwys. 2 and 97.

Woodland Park Zoological Gardens' Rose Garden, Seattle, Washington

At Ohme Gardens, more than a thousand trees, planted amid craggy rock outcroppings and softened by carpets of alpine plants and placid mountain pools, have turned nine barren hilltop acres into a green oasis. In all, some 50 kinds of plants may be found in the Gardens. Paths of native stone lead visitors up the hillside, past waterfalls, fern-bordered pools and rustic shelters. The elevated site offers a spectacular vista that includes Wenatchee Valley, the Columbia River and the Cascade Mountains.

For the purpose of creating a private retreat for their family, Herman Ohme and his wife began gardening on the hill in 1929. The Gardens opened to the public in 1939, and today Gordon Ohme continues to build on the efforts of his parents.

 P

Wisconsin

Boerner Botanical Gardens in Whitnall Park

5879 South 92nd St.	(414) 425-1130
Hales Corners,	529-1870
WI 53130	(for tour reservations)

Hours: mid–Apr. to Oct., every day 8–sunset; Nov. to mid–Apr., Mon.–Fri. 8–4.
Directions: located in the southwest section of Milwaukee County; Whitnall Park is about 2 mi. south of the intersection of I–894 and Hwy. 15, south of Grange Ave. and north of Rawson Ave.
Public Transportation: accessible by city bus (stop is about 3/4 mi. from the Gardens).

The Boerner Botanical Gardens, a major unit of the Milwaukee County Park System, display over 10,000 kinds of plants in the north-central section of the 660-acre Whitnall Park. Boerner's specialty gardens include the Herb Garden, Rose Garden (3,000 plants), Rock and Wildflower Garden, Bog Garden, Annual and Perennial Display Gardens, Peony Garden and Shrub Mall. Nature trails meander past woody plant collections, including dwarf shrubs, hedges, street trees, conifers, lilacs and shrub roses, as well as one of the finest and largest crabapple collections in the United States.

Land for the Park was acquired around 1930, and the Botanical Gardens were developed during that decade.

The University of Wisconsin Arboretum - Madison

1207 Seminole Hwy.   (608) 263-7888
Madison, WI 53711

Hours: grounds, every day 7 a.m. to 10 p.m.; MacKay Center, weekdays 9–4, weekends 12:30–4; closed holidays.
Admission: no fee.
Directions: located off Seminole Hwy., ¼ mi. north of its intersection with Hwys. 12, 14, 18 and 151; on the south edge of Madison.

The University of Wisconsin Arboretum is a complex of reconstructed plant and animal habitats, as well as horticultural collection areas. On the 1,270-acre site (600 acres open to the public), ecological microcosms and horticultural displays are connected by more than 20 miles of trails and fire lanes. Prairies, deciduous forests, conifer forests and wetlands form the various habitats, which include: Curtis Prairie (60 acres), the world's oldest restored tall-grass prairie; Greene Prairie (45 acres); and Noe Woods, a deciduous oak forest on 43 acres. The conifer forests include the Aldo Leopold Pines (59 acres) and Boreal Forest Plantings (14 acres).

Adhering to the more traditional concept of an Arboretum are the Longenecker Horticultural Gardens—50 acres, with collections arranged by genus and specialized groupings. Notable among these are the lilacs (230 species and varieties), flowering crabapples (135

Boerner Botanical Gardens in Whitnall Park, Milwaukee Park Commission, Education and Information Office, Hales Corner, Wisconsin (photo: Felton)

kinds), a small, formal shrub garden and the Pinetum, focusing on pines, spruces, firs and junipers. The Viburnum Garden, located on Manitou Way, contains more than 80 species and varieties of viburnums.

Development of the University of Wisconsin Arboretum began in the 1930s.

Mitchell Park Horticultural Conservatory

524 S. Layton Blvd.   (414) 278-4383
Milwaukee, WI 53215

Hours: Memorial Day to Labor Day, Mon.–Thurs. and weekends 9–8, Fri. 9–5; winter, Mon.–Fri. 9–5, weekends 9–8.
Admission: fee charged.
Directions: located at S. Layton Blvd. and W. Pierce St.
Public Transportation: accessible by city bus.

Three contemporary, 85 ft.-high glass domes form the Mitchell Park Conservatory, the star attraction of the 63-acre Park. Covering 2½ acres, the Conservatory shelters more than 3,200 kinds of plants. The tropical-garden house emphasizes colorful and economically important tropicals. The Arid Dome features over 1,000 species of desert plants. Displays in the third dome change five times a year to accommodate seasonal flowers. Just outside the Conservatory, the Sunken Gardens, containing waterlilies and other aquatic plants, is a featured summer attraction.

The original Mitchell Park Conservatory, built in the 1890s by the City Department of Parks, was razed in 1955, and the present Conservatory was erected from 1959 to 1964.

Paine Art Center and Arboretum

1410 Algoma Blvd.   (414) 235-4530
Oshkosh, WI 54901

Hours: Tues.–Sat. 10–4:30, Sun. 1–4:30; closed national holidays.
Admission: donation requested.
Directions: located in Oshkosh, 80 mi. north of Milwaukee; Hwy. 41 to Hwy. 110 (Algoma Blvd.); at the junction of Hwys. 110 and 21.

Fifteen acres surrounding the Paine Art Center comprise an arboretum that displays native and exotic trees, shrubs and herbaceous plants. The four acres immediately encircling the Center's manor house are patterned after 18th-century English gardens. In addition to the flower borders found here, an herb garden and rose garden are offered. Inside the Tudor-style mansion, visitors may examine the collection of paintings, as well as period furnishings. Across Algoma Boulevard, the Arboretum continues with a crabapple display, woodland and prairie.

Built in the 1920s, the estate was planned as the residence of Mr. and Mrs. Paine, but Mr. Paine died before it was completed. The Paine Art Center and Arboretum opened to the public in 1948.

Index